# *Stepping Out*
# *in Seattle*

## A Guide to Fun...
## for Singles, Couples and Friends

## 2nd Edition

## Mandy Johnston
### with
### Doug Feyereisen and Annie Goodgion

*Stepping Out in Seattle,* 2nd Edition.

ISBN 1-881409-21-X

Cover design by Megan Huston
Book design and layout by Gray Mouse Graphics

---

## DISCLAIMER

Although diligent efforts have been made to confirm the accuracy of information contained in this work, neither the publisher nor the author is responsible for errors or inaccuracies or for changes occurring after publication. This work was not prepared under the sponsorship, license, or authorization of any business, attraction, or organization described, depicted, or discussed herein.

---

JASI
Post Office Box 313
Medina, Washington 98039
(425) 454-3490 FAX: (425) 462-1335
Online Address: jasibooks@aol.com

Printed in the United States of America

Library of Congress Cataloging-in-Publication Data
Johnston, Mandy.
        Stepping out in Seattle/Mandy Johnston, with Doug Feyereisen and Annie Goodgion.—2nd ed.
p. cm.
 ISBN 1-881409-21-X
 1. Seattle (Wash.)——Guidebooks. I. Feyereisen, Doug, 1960–
II. Goodgion, Annie, 1962– . III Title.
F899.S43J65 1998
917.97'7720443—dc21                                                  97-35192
                                                                          CIP

# Table of Contents

# Introduction

The second edition of this popular guide to fun is long overdue. This expanded and revised edition includes more than 200 places to go and things to do. Use this book as a means to plan your playtime with someone special. This doesn't have to be your one true love; he or she can be your best friend. The purpose of *Stepping Out in Seattle* is to keep your life full of fun and to show you how to spend your weekend doing something besides sitting in front of the TV. Seattle and the surrounding area is a center of art, culture, music and great food! So, get out there and enjoy all there is to offer.

Of course, I can't promise you'll have the perfect date or day together, but I can suggest that you can follow in the well-trod paths of others and use this book to point you in the right direction. For the sake of a new, old, or yet-to-be-begun relationship, I hope you enjoy romantic candlelit dinners, a wild and woolly day of shopping together, chamber music, or a walk in the park. This book can be used to find the perfect spot to pop the question to your sweetheart or to relax over coffee with your college pal. Keep it handy when entertaining out-of-town guests to show them an insider's Seattle. Restaurants range from affordable to expensive, casual to formal, loud to quiet, so you can plan your evening accordingly.

I realize this book only scratches the surface of things to do and places to go in this wonderful region, and I welcome your comments and suggested additions. Please let me know what is "special" or "couple-friendly" about the recommendation. Maybe your favorite dating spot will find its way into the third edition!

Entries in this book are often marked with dollar signs ($) to help you plan an outing within your budget. Prices do change over time, so you should always call ahead if you're concerned about having enough cash on hand. However, the dollar signs will give you a general price range.

*Note:* the dollar sign is the cost for one person. In the restaurant section, the dollar signs represent an entrée price. The dollar signs value is as follows:

| | |
|---|---|
| $ | $10.00 or less |
| $$ | $20.00 or less |
| $$$ | $30.00 or less |
| $$$$ | $40.00 or less |
| $$$$$ | over $40.00 |

I hope you enjoy this second edition as much as I enjoyed the research and the writing of it. Have a great time together.

Mandy Johnston

# Chapter One

# Cultural Attractions

*W*hether you are in the mood for a little culture or a lot of culture, you can choose from many opportunities in our area. All of the arts are represented, including visual arts in galleries and museums, live theater, musical concerts, and more. Not every location in the city is mentioned, but here's a great place to start. The couples we sampled had their favorites, as will you.

# A Contemporary Theater (ACT)

*700 Union Street*
*Seattle*
*(206) 292-7676 (Box Office)*
*$$*

A Contemporary Theater—ACT—stages, you guessed it, contemporary plays. Generally, the focus is on the more recent playwrights. The mainstage season runs from May through November, but in December, ACT brings holiday audiences its legendary, popular version of Dickens' *A Christmas Carol*. This traditional Christmas tale makes a wonderful December date for people of all ages. ACT sometimes stages a winter production or two. The age range of the audience varies greatly, depending on the production, but is roughly mid-twenties to forty-plus. Half price tickets are available at the ACT box office for "day of" productions. Call for information on the current season and ticket prices.

# *Almost Live!*

*KING 5 Building*
*333 Dexter Avenue N*
*Seattle*
*(206) 421-5555*
*www.king5.com*

Anyone who loves to laugh, and loves the Pacific Northwest, will find being a part of the studio audience of *Almost Live!* a great dating idea. This hilarious (local) late-night comedy show airs on Channel 5, KING Television and has also been picked up by The Comedy Network on cable. The show is taped at the KING 5 studios in Seattle on weekend afternoons and evenings. Tickets are free but you must be at least sixteen years old. You can reserve up to four tickets, so make it a double date with your best friend. You will want to call first to find out what dates and times are available, reserve your space, then plan to be early because the seating is on a first come, first served basis. *Almost Live!* makes for a relaxed, fun, and free date. For more information and to reserve your tickets, call KING 5's *Almost Live!* line.

# BDA (Bellevue Downtown Association)

*500 198th Avenue NE (Suite 210)*
*Koll Building/Downtown Bellevue*
*(425) 453-1223 (information)*

The Bellevue Downtown Association keeps Bellevue hopping with interesting, entertaining and cultural events. The noontime *On the Town* concerts are held in various downtown plazas July and August; if you both work in Bellevue, make a date for lunch and music. The BDA also brings us the *Bellevue Arts and Crafts Weekend.* This multifair event—one of the most prestigious of its kind in the Northwest—takes place in and around Bellevue Square the last weekend in July and is an ideal date for art lovers. A variety of fascinating arts booths fills the streets during the *Pacific Northwest Arts and Crafts Fair. The Taste of Bellevue* at the 6th Street Fair will take care of mealtimes between browsing through the stalls. *The Bellevue Jazz Festival* is held the second weekend in July, and takes place at Bellevue Community College. During the months of November and December, enjoy *Bellevue: The Magic Season.* This celebration includes an ice-rink, a laser show, shopping, and other festivities. If you'd like to do a little "winter nibbling on the arts," consider the many events held during *Art Grazing* week, a potpourri of culinary, visual and performing arts held the last week in January.

# Belle Arte Concerts

*11100 NE 6th*
*Meydenbauer Center*
*Downtown Bellevue*
*(425) 454-2410 (ticket line)*

One of the Eastside's most successful home-grown arts organizations is Belle Arte Concerts, a chamber music series with a difference. For over a decade it has been the only chamber music series which presents regular programs. Although local and regional artists are prominently featured in many concerts, recent seasons have also included performances by celebrated musicians from throughout the world, such as the Shostakovich String Quartet from Russia.

As if fine music weren't enough, Belle Arte also offers its patrons ample free parking at the beautiful Meydenbauer Center, an art exhibit, and an elegant complimentary post-concert buffet with an opportunity to meet internationally acclaimed musicians.

Tickets are available by calling the Belle Arte ticket line. All performances are held at 7:30 P.M., and usually are held on Sunday evenings. It's a good idea to plan ahead since the concerts frequently sell out at least two weeks in advance.

# Bellevue Art Museum

*Third Floor, Bellevue Square*
*Downtown Bellevue*
*(425) 454-3322*

BAM, as Eastsiders refer to it, may be located in a trendy shopping mall, but it is a serious museum, and a pleasant surprise. BAM's prime directive is "to advance the excellence of Northwest art and crafts through a program of exhibition, education and publication." The exhibits change frequently, and cover the subjects of architecture, crafts, drawing, painting, photography, sculpture, textiles. Traveling shows and exhibits sometimes range outside the Northwestern arts community or feature local artists with an international following. Look for regional artists at "The Pacific Annual." You can pick up an exhibition schedule, or call for details.

The museum hours are from 10:00 A.M. to 6:00 P.M. Monday, Wednesday, Thursday and Saturday; 10:00 A.M. to 8:00 P.M. Tuesday and Friday; and 11:00 A.M. to 5:00 P.M. Sunday. The gift shop is open from 9:30 A.M. to 9:30 P.M. Monday through Saturday. BAM gladly accepts your personal check. Admission for BAM members is free. Every Tuesday is free admission for all ages (donations welcome). After visiting the museum, try one of the mall restaurants for a nice dinner or a drink. Marie Callender's and Jake O'Shaughnessey's are good options, and both have lounges that come alive in the evening.

## The Bellevue Repertory Theater

*606 110th Avenue NE/Suite 211*
*Bellevue*
*(425) 454-5025*

The Bellevue Repertory Theater, established more than 10 years ago, is the first Equity professional theater group on the Eastside. The Rep stages a great *Shakespeare in the Grass* series at Bellevue Place and at Chateau Ste. Michelle. Its new theater home is at Meydenbauer Center in downtown Bellevue.

Cucina! Cucina! offers a great box supper deal for performances at Bellevue Place; you order your meal with your tickets. The food is a cut above your ordinary picnic fare, and the prices are good. Beverages are available in the courtyard where the performances are held.

You can order tickets from the Bellevue Rep. Prices are from $8.00 to $10.00 and the dinners are form $5.00 to $8.00. Those who love Shakespeare, and who want to support this Equity theater company, will certainly enjoy these authentic, outdoor productions.

## BOOKSTORES

Although there are many, many outstanding bookstores in the greater Seattle area, here are a few that have more to offer than just books. They all have a café of some type and special events, such as lectures and book signings. However, don't rule out your favorite neighborhood bookstore just because it wasn't listed here!

## Barnes & Noble Booksellers

Browsing through a bookstore on a rainy day makes a great outing, and Barnes & Noble is one of the best bookstore chains around. Wandering through the bookshelves and discussing likes and dislikes in literature can teach you a lot about each other. The bookstores of today look more like a library/espresso bar, so take advantage! Barnes & Noble is a large chain, with over 150,000 titles, so you're sure to find all the books on your list. Curl up in a cozy chair and read poetry to each other (very romantic and very inexpensive).

Barnes & Noble is open every day from 9:00 A.M. until 11:00 P.M., so you can go whenever the mood strikes you!

Barnes & Noble locations:
  15600 NE 8th, Crossroads Mall, Bellevue (425) 644-1650
  626 106th NE, Bellevue (425) 451-8463
  Pickering Place, Issaquah (425) 557-8808
  2700 NE University Village Mall, Seattle (206) 517-4107

## Borders Books & Music

*1501 4th*
*Seattle*
*(206) 622-4599*

Borders Books is another fabulous bookstore to explore, with a wide selection of books and tapes. Part of a large chain with over 200,000 titles, This bookstore will satisfy any avid reader. There is also a coffee shop within the store called Cafe Espresso. You can stop book browsing and have a steamy conversation over a steaming cup of java!

Borders Books is open from 8:00 A.M. to 10:00 P.M. Monday through Thursday, 9:00 A.M. to 11:00 P.M. Friday and Saturday, and 9:00 A.M. to 9:00 P.M. Sunday. The coffee shop keeps the same hours, so you can make this trip a morning or evening date.

## Elliott Bay Book Company

*Elliott Bay Cafe (downstairs)*
*101 S Main Street*
*Pioneer Square/Seattle*
*Bookstore: (206) 624-6600*
*Cafe: (206) 682-6664*

The Elliott Bay Book Company offers a unique way to spend "quality" time together. The bookstore itself is a fun place to explore. It's unlikely you won't find something you want to read among the thousands of titles (backlist and new) that fill the shelves to overflowing. If you can't locate that special book, they'll order it for you. The Elliott Bay Book Company is open from 10:00 A.M. to

11:00 P.M., Monday through Saturday, and noon to 6:00 P.M. on Sundays.

Downstairs, there's a great little café. The tables are surrounded by tall bookshelves, accentuating the "intellectual" mood. Choose from sandwich-and-soup type meals, coffee, espresso and tea, and wines by the glass. The café is open from 7:00 A.M. to 10:30 P.M. Monday through Friday, from 10:00 A.M. to 10:30 P.M. on Saturday, and from 11:00 to 5:30 P.M. on Sundays.

Besides visiting the bookstore and cozy café, you might consider attending one of the continuous string of readings by famous authors. Readings begin at 7:30 P.M. (unless otherwise specified) and a variety of subjects is represented. A monthly listing is available. For more information, call (206) 624-6600, or stop by the store. The majority of the readings are free, but a few special guest speakers require advance tickets (usually about $5.00). Reservations go quickly for well-known authors.

# The Burke Memorial Washington State Museum

*University Of Washington*
*17th Avenue NE & NE 45th Street*
*Seattle*
*(206) 543-5590 (recorded information)*
*www.edu\burkemuseum*
*$*

Learn more about Seattle at the new Burke Museum. The focus here is natural and cultural history. Filled with powerful images of Pacific and Northwest Coast cultures, Burke Museum underwent an eight-month renovation before opening its new exhibition galleries in November, 1997. The Pacific Voices exhibit showcases 17 Pacific Rim cultures strongly represented in the Puget Sound area. It is a profoundly moving exhibit and will touch the heart of Seattle natives and visitors alike. You can also take a trek through history at the *Life and Times of Washington State* exhibit, where you'll learn about our state's natural history.

The Burke Museum is located in the Northwest corner of the University of Washington campus. The museum is open daily from 10:00 A.M. to 5:00 P.M., and until 8:00 P.M. on Thursday. Admission is free to all museum members and UW students and staff.

# 5th Avenue Theatre

*1308 5th Avenue*
*Downtown Seattle*
*(206) 625-1900( Box Office) or (206) 292-ARTS*
*$$-$$$*

Impress your date with tickets to a musical at the 5th Avenue Theatre. This genre has made a strong comeback in Seattle, and the 5th Avenue is largely responsible. Originally built in 1926 as a vaudeville house, it was remodeled in 1980. The theater's architectural design recreates the throne room from ancient China's Forbidden City in Beijing. Surrounded by this magical setting, you will be treated to a wonderful production. The mission of the 5th Avenue Theatre is to preserve the historic, architectural and cultural enrichment of Seattle. A total of four shows are presented each year, some locally produced and others touring productions. The themes and shows cover the gamut of light opera and musical comedy. Nearly all the old favorites have been—or will be—staged and, at least once per season, the theater offers one of the big hits from the New York or London theater scenes. The 5th Avenue brings in big stars such as Julie Andrews, performing her famous role in *Victor, Victoria!*

Dress is typically on the dressy side, depending on what night and performance you choose. The subject matter determines the age of the audience. During intermission, you can refresh with coffee, sodas, pastries or a selection from the bar. There are restaurants within walking distance (see Duke's Fish House, the Palm Court and The Garden Court at the Olympic Hotel in chapter 2, *Restaurants*). Ticket prices vary depending on the show and location of the seats, and are available through Ticketmaster (206) 292-2787 or in person at the 5th Avenue Box Office (Hours: 9:30 A.M. to 5:00 P.M., Monday through Thursday).

# Frye Art Museum

*704 Terry Street*
*Capitol Hill*
*Seattle*
*(206) 622-9250*

Add a touch of culture and style to your life, without spending a lot of money, at the Frye Art Museum. A few hours at the Frye combined with an espresso or glass of wine at the Gallery Cafe can be a great date. The museum has undergone an extensive renovation and expansion, but still has an intimate ambiance. The architecture is absolutely incredible! The works displayed are late 19th Century and 20th Century, European and American Representational Art.

The Frye sponsors concerts, workshops, lectures and readings. Seating is limited, and passes are available at the front desk one hour before shows. Thursday evenings include dinner at the Gallery Cafe, from 5:00 P.M. to 7:30 P.M., and that night the gallery is open until 9:00 P.M. For a truly sophisticated date, have tea at the Frye any Thursday from 2:00 P.M. to 5:00 P.M. A combination of tea and art makes for a very classy date! Complete your evening with a postcard or poster of your favorite painting, as a reminder of your time together.

The traveling shows—ranging from traditional to modern—change every month. You can pick up a free newsletter at the desk or add your name to the mailing list. Attendance is free of charge, which is a real bonus if you are on a tight budget. (Cash donations are accepted, and it's a nice way to support the arts.) The Frye Art Museum is open from 10:00 A.M. to 5:00 P.M. Tuesday through Saturday, from 10:00 A.M. to 9:00 P.M. Thursdays, and from 12:00 noon to 5:00 P.M. Sundays.

# Gallery Walk in Pioneer Square

*Pioneer Square/Seattle*

The first Thursday gallery opening and walk is a cultural event, a see-and-be-seen opportunity, and a sort of mini Mardi Gras. Participating galleries from the Pike Place Market to the Kingdome—and especially in the Pioneer Square area—are open special hours from 6:00 P.M. to 8:00 P.M. The adjacent bars, pubs and restaurants are also ready and waiting for art-lovers ready to take a break. Art patrons and browsers alike from all over the Seattle area take advantage of this special evening. Dress is casual, although many people show up after work. If this is your plan, be sure to bring a comfortable pair of shoes.

If you are in a serious relationship, buying art together is a special experience. But besides viewing the art, this is a terrific people-watching event. Some of the more dramatically artistic outfits show up at the gallery openings! The age ranges from twenty to sixty-plus, and the crowd can get very large (even on rainy days). End the evening at one of the nearby drinking and dining establishments in Pioneer Square; there are many options, ranging from wild and funky to elegant and quiet, or even bohemian and artsy.

Kirkland also has a Gallery Walk of its own. For more information, see the *Noteworthy Neighborhood* section in chapter 4.

# Henry Art Gallery

*15th NE and NE 41st*
*University of Washington*
*Seattle*
*(206) 543-2280 (museum)*
*(206) 545-9239 (gallery shop)*

Located at the western edge of the University of Washington, the small Henry Art Gallery focuses on contemporary art. Both international and national exhibits are featured. One thing about modern art, it always gives you something to talk about. You can call the museum ahead of time to see what is currently on display and how *avant garde* it might be. The Henry Art Gallery has undergone a major renovation, so if you haven't seen it lately, go now! There is also a gallery bookstore and poster shop. Admission for all University students and staff is free and Thursdays are free to everyone. The museum hours are from 10:00 A.M. to 5:00 P.M. on Tuesday, Thursday, Saturday and Sunday; 10:00 A.M. to 8:00 P.M. on Wednesday and Thursday; and closed on Monday.

# Intiman Theater-Playhouse

*201 Mercer Street*
*Seattle Center*
*Lower Queen Anne*
*(206) 269-1900*
*$$*

For an intimate evening, try a good play. Located on the Seattle Center grounds, the theater is small (424 seats) and has a cozy, cultured atmosphere. The productions and sets are beautiful, and the plays are sure to stimulate the intellect and give you plenty to discuss. *Peter Pan* is an annual tradition. The audience will vary depending on the play, but college age and then thirty to fifty-plus make up the majority of the audiences.

The season runs from May to December. Ticket are available through Ticketmaster (206) 292-2787 and the Intiman box office. There are other options, however. Ticket/Ticket (206) 324-2744 sells them the day of the performance at reduced prices. The Intiman also has "pay what you can" performances. The minimum is $1.00, and these tickets sell fast, so call for more information on the dates of those shows.

# Japanese Garden and Tea Ceremony

*Washington Park Arboretum, Lake Washington Boulevard E*
*North of E Madison Street*
*Seattle*
*(206) 684-4725*
*$*

After lunch or a picnic in the Arboretum, a romantic stroll through the beautiful Japanese Garden can top off a wonderful afternoon. The Japanese Garden recreates a compressed mini-scape of mountains, forests, lakes, tablelands and village. It is so peaceful and serene, you will find visiting it a very soothing experience. Wander through this enchanted garden, learning about the Japanese use of color, symbolism and tradition, or just enjoy the quiet beauty. You'll encounter goldfish ponds and the authentic Tea House. Chado—The Way of Tea—is demonstrated on the third Saturday of each month, and is included with your admission fee.

You can take part in this ancient Japanese ritual April through October, at 1:30 P.M.

The Japanese Garden is open seven days a week, March 1 through November 30, from 10:00 A.M. to closing. (Closing time varies with the season). The summer hours are from 10:00 A.M. to 8:00 P.M. and the garden is closed from December through February.

## Museum of Flight

*9404 E Marginal Way S*
*Seattle*
*(206)764-5720 (visitor information)*
*(206)764-5712, ext. 62 (tours)*
*$*

For those intrigued by the world of flight or just fascinated with learning new things, the Museum of Flight is a great destination. Explore the history of aviation, climb inside a cockpit, and trace the steps to space exploration. The museum is open seven days a week and the hours are from 10:00 A.M. to 5:00 P.M. daily and until 9:00 P.M. on Thursday. Admission is free the first Thursday of each month, from 5:00 P.M. to 9:00 P.M.

After exploring the museum, make your way over to the east side of Boeing Field (7299 Airport Way South) and have a meal or a drink at the Blue Max Restaurant and Lounge. Located in the Passenger Terminal at Boeing King County Airport, the Blue Max is a great aviation fan's hangout. Both restaurant and lounge overlook the activity at Boeing Field. The funky bar atmosphere is a lot of fun (for couples over twenty-one years old), and features theme drinks and daily specials. There's dancing after 9:00 P.M. on Friday and Saturday, Happy Hour dollar busters, free hot food buffets, and more.

Just north of the terminal, The Aviator's Store is the perfect place to shop for a gift or souvenir related to the world of pilots and planes. The Aviator's Store (phone (206) 763-0666) is open from 9:00 A.M. to 6:00 P.M. Monday through Friday; from 9:00 A.M. to 5:00 P.M. on Saturday; and from 10:00 A.M. to 5:00 P.M. on Sunday.

# Museum of History and Industry

*2700 24th E*
*Montlake area, South of the UW Stadium*
*Seattle*
*(206) 324-1126 (recorded information) or (206) 324-1125*
*$*

A rainy day is the perfect time to head for the Museum of History and Industry. As you wander through the permanent exhibits of Seattle and Pacific Northwest history, you'll learn many little-known facts about the city and the region. The main exhibits change about every three to five months, so you might want to call ahead to find out what is currently on display.

Admission is charged daily except Tuesdays, when a donation only is requested. The museum is open from 10:00 A.M. to 5:00 P.M. daily, and is closed Thanksgiving, Christmas, and New Year's Day. They will accept your personal check.

The pleasant paths and trails along Lake Washington and into the Arboretum connect at the museum, so you can add a little natural history to your day. Bring walking shoes, and maybe an umbrella.

# The Pacific Northwest Ballet (PNB)

*Seattle Opera House*
*301 Mercer Street/ between 3rd and 4th*
*Seattle Center/Seattle*
*(206) 441-9411(general information)*

The Seattle Opera House is home to our premier ballet company, the Pacific Northwest Ballet. The season runs from September through June, and the Company presents six programs per year. Included in every season is *The Nutcracker*. This Seattle tradition makes a wonderful holiday-time experience. Anyone who loves beautiful music and the grace of ballet will enjoy dressing up for a special evening of dinner and a PNB performance. The age of the audiences varies, depending on the ballet and the show time. Tickets are available through the box office or through Ticketmaster. Prices vary, depending on the seats, days and time of performance.

## Rosalie Whyel Museum of Doll Art

*1116 108th Avenue NE*
*Bellevue*
*(425) 455-1116*
*www.dollart.com/dollart/*
*$*

Stroll down memory lane while making new memories at this beautiful museum. You'll travel back in time to your own childhood as you enjoy the collection of dolls, toys, teddy bears and childhood memorabilia. The museum store is full of keepsake items for you and your friend or date to remember your day together. This museum isn't just a "girlie-date." Men will also recall special childhood toys as you wander the museum.

The museum is open 10:00 A.M. to 5:00 P.M. Monday through Saturday, and from 1:00 P.M. to 5:00 P.M. Sunday. Admission is very reasonable, so treat your date to dinner in one of Bellevue's great downtown restaurants. (See chapter 2, *Restaurants*, for ideas).

## Seattle Art Museum

*100 University Street*
*Downtown Seattle*
*(206) 654-3100*
*$*

The Seattle Art Museum is a great place to spend time together, especially if you both love art. The building is nearly as spectacular as the collections, and was the subject of considerable controversy during its construction. There are also state-of-the-art educational alcoves with videotapes, if you really want to get into the subject. (You can learn a lot about a person by finding out his/her tastes in art.) The exhibits change, so you will want to call and find out what is on display. There are also special activities such as the authentic Tea Ceremony, that are available by reservation only.

The museum is open from 11:00 A.M. to 5:00 P.M. Tuesday through Saturday; from 11:00 A.M. to 9:00 P.M. Thursday; and from noon to 5:00 P.M. on Sunday (closed Mondays). Admission is free the first Thursday of every month. The museum accepts all major credit cards and personal checks. The deli on the main floor serves sandwiches and salads. Or you can just pause for a beverage break, and sip coffee, soft drinks, juices, beer or wine before exploring the museum.

## Seattle Asian Art Museum

*1400 E Prospect*
*Volunteer Park/Capitol Hill*
*Seattle*
*(206) 654-3100 (recording)*
*(206) 625-8900 (information)*

Located in Seattle's beautiful Volunteer Park, the Seattle Asian Art Museum makes a unique and enjoyable destination. The museum highlights a collection of art from Japan, China, Korea, India, Himalaya and Southwest Asia. There is also a very romantic Tea Garden to explore together. The museum store offers wonderful keepsake items for you and your date or friend. Pack a lunch and have a picnic in the park before, or after, you explore the museum.

The museum is open from 10:00 A.M. to 5:00 P.M. Tuesday through Sunday, and from 10:00 A.M. to 9:00 P.M. Thursday. Thanks to the generous support of Boeing, admission is free the first Thursday of every month. If used within one week, your ticket to the Seattle Asian Museum is good for free admission to the Seattle Art Museum.

## Seattle Opera

*300 Mercer Street/between 3rd and 4th*
*Seattle Center*
*Lower Queen Anne/Seattle*
*(206) 389-7600 (general information)*
*$$*

A night at the opera is a classy experience for all ages. The Seattle Opera series runs from August through May at the Opera House in the Seattle Center, and the following year's operas are announced in November. The English subtitles will help you understand exactly what is happening on stage. Founded in 1964, the Seattle Opera stages both traditional and contemporary works, including Wagner's *Der Ring des Nibelungen*—which was first performed in Seattle in 1975, and has drawn audiences from around the world.

The building's architecture is beautiful, elegant and romantic. During intermission, you can enjoy delicious desserts, soft drinks, wine and champagne or espressos. Evening performances begin at 7:30 P.M. and the Sunday matinées begin at 2:00 P.M. The opera starts promptly, so if you are planning dinner out pre-performance, be on time. Single performance or season tickets are available by mail or from the Opera House ticket office.

## Seattle Symphony

*Opera House/Seattle Center*
*Offices: 4th floor/Seattle Center House*
*(206) 443-4747(ticket office)*
*$$–$$$$*

If music is the way to the heart of your loved one, why not spend and afternoon or evening at the Seattle Symphony. The Symphony usually calls the Opera House home, but they also hold special performances in other locations around the area (such as Chateau Ste. Michelle winery and the Moore Theater). The season runs from September through June, with performances weekly. Concerts vary from classical to pop, with a special *Discover Music* series for people with kids. Find out what composer or instrument your companion likes, then call the Seattle Symphony for suggestions. Make an evening of it, with dinner downtown first. Ticket prices vary depending on the performance and seats.

## Summer Nights at the Pier

*Piers 62 and 63*
*Waterfront/Elliott Bay*
*Seattle*
*(206) 281-8111 (information)*
*(206) 628-0888 (ticket line)*
*www.summernights.org*
*$-$$*

Summer nights are wonderful in and of themselves, but during July and August, they can be even more fun if you share them with friends on the Seattle waterfront. Sponsored by Magnolia Hi-Fi and AT&T, *Summer Nights at the Pier* is a concert series which takes place on Piers 62 and 63—on Alaskan Way, overlooking Elliott Bay. The setting is spectacular; the view of Puget Sound and West Seattle is stunning. The concerts are timed to catch the sunset, which makes the setting even more breathtaking. The series includes all kinds of music, from oldies to current pop. The box office is located in front of the pier and the hours are from 11:00 A.M. to 6:00 P.M., Tuesday through Sunday (closed on Monday). The ticket prices range from show to show, and there is a surcharge if you buy your tickers the day of the concert. You can pay with Visa, Mastercard, personal check or cash.

## Ticket/Ticket

*(206) 324-2744*
*401 Broadway E*
*Broadway Market (2nd level)*
*Validated parking in the Broadway Market Garage*
*$–$$$*

*1st & Pike*
*Pike Place Market Information Booth*
*Validated parking in the Public Market Parking Garage*

If your evening includes seeing a show but you're a little short of cash, go to Ticket/Ticket. With two convenient locations, This vendor sells half-price tickets the day of the show* for theater, music and dance events. Included are tickets to The Backstage, Bathhouse, Broadway Performance Hall, Comedy Underground,

Empty Space, Intiman, Jazz Alley, New City, New Image Theater, Pioneer Square Theater, Seattle Choral Company, Seattle Mime Theater, Seattle Opera and Seattle Symphony as well as others. Prices vary, depending on the show.

Ticket/Ticket is a walk-up service only, and accepts cash only. The hours are from 10:00 A.M. to 7:00 P.M., Tuesday through Saturday, and noon to 6:00 P.M. at Broadway; from noon to 6:00 P.M., Tuesday through Sunday at Pike Place. Ticket/Ticket makes it possible for everyone to see a good show, for a good price! They also sell coupon books, if you want to give that special someone a broad hint.

*Matinee tickets are sold the day before and day of, and Monday tickets are sold on Sunday.

## University of Washington Arts Tickets Office

*4001 University Way*
*University District*
*Seattle*
*(206) 543-4880*
*$-$$*

The University of Washington stages a number of plays and musical and dance productions, offering a nice evening's entertainment. The UW also hosts a variety of touring groups. You can purchase tickets at the UW Arts ticket office, or at the theater on the night of the show. For information on what is playing and ticket prices, call the box office at (206) 543-4880. The ticket office is open from 10:30 A.M. to 4:30 P.M. Monday through Friday, during the summer, and from 10:30 A.M. to 6:00 P.M. during the academic year.

You can also call the individual theaters: Meany Theater (206) 685-2742, Glenn Hughes Playhouse (206) 543-5646, and Penthouse (206) 543-5638. Prices vary, depending on the production. Typically the age range of the audience is college age and from twenty-eight to thirty-something, but it depends on the show.

# Village Theatre

*303 Front Street N*
*Issaquah*
*(425) 392-2202*
*www.vt.org*

Music can make your heart sing, so why not take someone special to a musical at the Village Theatre in picturesque Issaquah? The Village Theatre provides something for everyone, including comic musicals such as *Little Shop of Horrors*, traditional favorites such as *Fiddler on the Roof*, and classics such as *Carousel, Seven Brides for Seven Brothers* and *Bells Are Ringing*. The theater itself, nestled in beautiful downtown Issaquah, has a small, intimate feel. Before or after the show, try one of the many restaurants in the area, or just enjoy the scenic drive along Interstate 90. The Village Theatre is a nonprofit arts organization committed to excellence in family theater.

Ticket prices range, depending on seats and time of show, so call the ticket office for more information. Subscriptions for five shows is a great deal for music lovers of all ages. The ticket office is open from 11:00 A.M. to 7:00 P.M., Tuesday through Saturday.

# Chapter 2

# Restaurants

*C*hoosing the perfect restaurant is an essential part of a great night together. Where, and what, you eat can set the mood for the entire evening. There are several things to consider when choosing a restaurant. First, what kind of food do you like? This is a matter of personal preference, and I can't begin to suggest what type of food you should eat. However, this chapter gives you a wide selection of food from around the world.

Second, how much money do you want to spend? This is a practical, but important consideration. After all, no one is impressed by a date who can't pay for the dinner! You'll find all restaurants in this chapter clearly marked with dollar signs ($) to help you find an acceptable price range.

Finally, what kind of ambiance are you seeking? The restaurants in this chapters are divided into four categories: casual, loud and lively, romantic, and sophisticated. The first three are self-explanatory, but the sophisticated category may confuse you. The restaurants listed there are places to "see and be seen," where the food is great, the atmosphere can range from funky to trendy, and the crowd is hip!

*Bon appetite!*

# CASUAL RESTAURANTS

## Angel's Thai Cuisine
*235 Broadway E*
*Seattle*
*(206) 328-0515*
*$*

Those who appreciate Thai food, or like trying new cuisine, will want to stop in at Angel's Thai. When you walk in, you can watch as the food is prepared in the open kitchen. The food is authentic Thai, but the restaurant has been Americanized. If you've never tried Thai food, this is the perfect place to try it out. The noise level includes kitchen sounds, as well as quiet music. The age of diners ranges from twenty to fifty-plus. Angel's is open from 11:30 A.M. to 10:30 P.M. Monday through Thursday; 11:30 A.M. to 11:00 P.M. Friday; 12:00 noon to 11:00 P.M. Saturday; and 12:00 noon to 10:00 P.M. Sunday. The restaurant accepts major credit cards, but no personal checks.

## Benjamin's on Lake Union
*809 Fairview Place N*
*Seattle*
*(206) 621-8262*
*$$*

Benjamin's sits right on picturesque Lake Union, looking toward Gas Works Park. At night, the reflection of the lights shimmering on the lake is breathtaking. The atmosphere at Benjamin's is casual and relaxed. The great location makes this a great place to eat before a night out on the town. The bar is perfect for post-theater drinks. The food features a variety of Northwest favorites including fresh seafood, chicken, salads, pasta and steaks from the open-flame display kitchen. Both the restaurant and the bar are very popular, and at night, the lounge hops. There is outdoor seating during the warm summer months. Every Sunday, Benjamin's features an award-winning brunch—a great way to start a Sunday together.

Benjamin's serves dinner from 4:30 P.M. to 10:00 P.M. every evening. The popular restaurant does recommend reservations for dinner and weekday lunch.

# Bill's Off Broadway

*725 E Pine Street*
*Capitol Hill*
*(206) 323-7200*
*$*

A pizza place for true pizza lovers, Bill's Off Broadway serves up some of the best pizza in town. A variety of "classic" pasta entrées is also available. The interior is rustic, with rough-hewn wood walls and wooden tables and chairs. The atmosphere is definitely casual. You can watch the pizzas being made as you walk in the door. Bill's serves every pizza under the sun, from plain cheese to The Big 13 (you guessed it, 13 toppings). If you can't agree on toppings, try one of the mini-pizzas. A television set brings you big sporting events, and there is a small adjoining bar. The typical age range is from twenty to forty-plus.

This is a good spot for a casual evening out. The Egyptian Theater is right across the street (see page 140) and Bill's is open late, if you have an after-the-movie-pizza-attack. Hours are: Monday through Thursday 11:00 A.M. to 12:00 A.M., Friday 11:00 A.M. to 1:00 A.M., Saturday 12:00 A.M. to 1:00 A.M., and Sunday 12:00 noon to 12:00 A.M. Bill's accepts Visa, Mastercard, American Express and personal checks, and validates parking in the Seattle Community College Garage right across the street. No reservations necessary.

# Burgermaster Drive-Ins

*10606 NE Northup Way*
*Bellevue/Kirkland border*
*(425) 827-9566*

*9820 Aurora Avenue N*
*North Seattle*
*(206) 522-2044*
*$*

Burgermaster is a drive-in reminiscent of years gone by. These locations are the only Burgermasters with car service—a legendary dating stop-off for couples from the '30s to the '60s. The romantic appeal comes from having your own private dining room (your car) and your favorite tape, or CD, playing in the background (in the "old days," it was your radio, of course). Burgermaster provides an inexpensive and delicious dinner served on a window tray hooked to the side of your car. Big, juicy burgers can be special-ordered with all the condiments you like (watch those onions!).

The service stalls are filled with cars whose occupants range from sixteen to sixty-plus. Sixteen year-olds will enjoy showing off their new car, and sixty year-olds will feel sixteen again. Burgermaster is open from 7:00 A.M. to 2:00 A.M., Monday through Friday, and from 10:00 A.M. to 2:00 A.M. Saturday and Sunday. The late-night hours make Burgermaster a great place to go after a movie.

Note: Other Burgermasters (without the drive-in feature) are located in:
*Plaza:* 9749 Holman Road NW (206) 784-2360
*Lynnwood:* 18411 Highway 99 (425) 774-5831
*University:* 3042 NE 4th (206) 525-7100

# Cactus

*4220 E Madison*
*Madison Park/Seattle*
*(206) 324-4140*
*$$*

Cactus serves up delicious Mexican and the Southwest food. The brightly colored decor includes painted tables and a tapas bar. The atmosphere is casual, comfortable and fun. Located right in the middle of the Madison Park strip (see *Noteworthy Neighborhoods* in chapter 4 for more information on Madison Park), Cactus is a great date spot. You can pop into one of the many bars for an after-dinner drink, or take a stroll down to the park. The noise level is moderate, so you can talk without raising your voice. The age range is from mid-twenties and up, and the dress is casual.

Cactus serves dinner from 5:00 P.M. to 10:00 P.M. Monday through Thursday and Sunday, and from 5:00 P.M. to 10:30 P.M. Friday and Saturday. Reservations are honored.

# California Pizza Kitchen

*595 106th NE*
*Bellevue*
*(425) 454-2545*
*$$*

The California Pizza Kitchen is not your ordinary pizza parlor. This lively and popular restaurant serves things such as Roasted Garlic Chicken, Moo Shu Chicken Calzone, and Shrimp Scampi, to name a few. Of course, for you traditionalists out there, try the Five-Cheese and Tomato or Pepperoni (made with homemade pepperoni) pizza. The California Pizza Kitchen also serves up delicious appetizers, salads, pasta and sandwiches. The atmosphere is casual. The restaurant's color scheme is black and yellow, with lots of windows and mirrors. It makes a great pre-or post-movie spot.

The California Pizza Kitchen opens at 11:00 A.M. Monday through Saturday and closes at 10:00 P.M. Monday through Thursday, 11:00 P.M. Friday and Saturday., Sunday hours are from noon to 9:00 P.M. You don't need reservations at the California Pizza Kitchen, but expect a wait. When you arrive, put your name on the waiting list and receive a beeper from the host/hostess. They'll "beep" you when your table is ready. Very "California."

## Chandler's Crabhouse and Fresh Fish Market

*901 Fairview Avenue N*
*Southeast Lake Union*
*(206) 223-2722*
*$$*

Located on Lake Union, Chandler's Crabhouse is designed much like the Farmer's Market in The Pike Place Market. The casual atmosphere and view of the lake and boats makes it a great choice for an evening of good food and casual conversation. The restaurant can get noisy, not with music, but with the sounds of loud talking and laughter. Dress varies from casual to work attire, and the general look is "casually relaxed." As the name implies, Chandler's is famous for seafood. The menu changes regularly and includes "Guaranteed Signature Items," which are guaranteed to please or are "on the house."

The crowd is made up of a variety of ages, but is mainly composed of the early to mid-thirties. Chandler's is proud to have been voted by the Bite of Seattle '92 as the restaurant with "Seattle's Best Crab Cakes." Look for them on the menu, both as a starter, and as an entrée.

The bar serves mostly as an after-work spot, and is almost part of the restaurant. Dinner is served every night until 11:00 P.M. The bar closes, "when everyone leaves!" Smoking tables are available upon request. Reservations are strongly suggested for weekend nights and weekday lunch. Free parking is available in the Chandler Cove parking garage.

## Charlie's

*217 Broadway E*
*Seattle*
*(206) 323-2535*
*$*

Stepping into Charlie's makes you feel as if you've entered a time warp. This hip restaurant attracts all ages from eighteen to sixty. (The bar tends to be made up of people age twenty-one to fifty.) Charlie's also serves very late, which makes it a popular late-night spot. Head here after a movie for a late-night snack, or to have dessert and coffee. Dress ranges from casual to dressy. The menu selections are classic "American," meaning steaks, roast beef, pasta, salads, etc. Charlie's accepts credit cards and personal checks, and reservations are not necessary. Dinner is served until 2:00 A.M. Monday through Thursday, until 3:00 A.M. on Friday and until 1:00 A.M. Saturday and Sunday.

## Chili's Grill & Bar

*Crossroads Shopping Center*
*Bellevue*
*(425) 641-0500*
*$-$$*

Chili's is a national restaurant chain that still manages to serve great food and provide excellent service. A variety of dishes are offered, all with a Southwestern flavor. Try one of Chili's salads, burgers or chicken dishes. The bar serves a full menu and there's always a game on the TV. Chili's is conveniently located near the Crossroads Cinema, so it makes a great pre-movie dinner spot. Or, stop by after the movie for a bite to eat, and try the Awesome Blossom (which is one incredible plate of onion rings). You should also give their dessert menu a look-see. The atmosphere is relaxed, casual and fun. Dress is jeans, shorts or whatever.

Chili's serves dinner until 10:00 P.M. on weekdays and until 11:00 P.M. on weekends. They don't take reservations, and there can be a wait on weekend nights. Make sure you show up early if plan to catch a movie after dining.

## Chinook's at Salmon Bay

*1900 W Nickerson Suite 103*
*Fishermen's Terminal/Seattle*
*(206) 283-4665*
*$$*

Chinook's at Salmon Bay is a fun stop for lunch or dinner. The restaurant is located in Fishermen's Terminal and has a view of the marina. The atmosphere is relaxed and casual dress is standard. You can dine at a window-front table, a booth with a view, at the counter for a quick bite, outside in the patio, or in the bar. The menu features fresh Pacific Northwest seafood, and everything is delicious. There are many options, and if you can't decide, try a seafood platter with selections from the menu. The restaurant is loud, a combination of talking and noise from the open kitchen. The bar opens into the restaurant, so on weekend nights (or during any Husky football game), it can add to the noise.

Speaking of Husky football, Chinook's loves Husky fans and hosts the Chinook's "Dawg Boat." The Dawg Boat leaves Fishermen's Terminal and cruises out to Husky Stadium. You don't have to fuss with parking at the stadium; instead parking is free at Fishermen's Terminal. You can enjoy breakfast before the cruise, or dinner afterward. Ticket prices include a complimentary beverage at Chinook's. For more information, call (206) 283-HOOK.

Chinook's at Salmon Bay serves dinner from 5:00 P.M. until 10:00 P.M. Sunday through Thursday, and from 5:00 P.M. to 11:00 P.M. Friday and Saturday.

## Cutter's Bayhouse

*2001 Western Avenue*
*Pike Place Market*
*(206) 448-4884*
*$$*

A perfect way to end a stroll through the Pike Place Market is a meal or drink at Cutter's Bayhouse. The restaurant looks out at Elliott Bay and beyond to Puget Sound. The atmosphere is light and lively, with an open kitchen and high ceilings. Cutter's 100 percent nonsmoking environment makes it a haven for those offended by cigarette smoke. Even the bar is full of fresh, clean air! The menu includes a little of everything, from salads to steaks, though seafood is a specialty and comes fresh from the nearby fish markets. Cutter's serves Tom Stockley's carefully selected wines.

Although you'll see all ages here, the crowd leans toward the young professional. The noise level does tend to rise quickly, especially on weekend nights. The bar is a very active place, and the sounds of conversation spill over into the busy restaurant. However, you can still carry on a conversation. Dinner is served until 11:00 P.M. and until 1:30 A.M. in the lounge. Parking is available in the Market Place garage and there is on-street parking as well. Reservations are strongly suggested. Cutter's accepts major credit cards and local checks.

## Duke's Restaurants

*Bar and Grilles: $$*
*Chowderhouses: $-$$*

The aim of the Duke's group of restaurants is to provide good food, good service, and a casual and fun place to hang out with your friends. The restaurants are classed by types (bar and grilles, chowder-houses and the fish house), and there are some differences which you may want to consider when making your plans. The restaurants accept major credit cards and personal checks.

The bar and grilles are located in Bellevue (23 Lake Bellevue Drive; (425) 455-5775) and Queen Anne (236 1st W; (206) 283-4400). The emphasis is on value, reasonable prices for good-size portions. The atmosphere is somewhat sports-oriented and the bars are almost always lively. The crowd is usually sophisticated and from thirty to fifty-plus. The menu offers everything from hamburgers to lobster. Reservations are suggested, especially for weekend dinners.

The chowder houses, located at Lake Union (901 Fairview N; (206) 382-9963) and Green Lake (7850 Green Lake Dr. N; (206) 522-4908), are a little more casual (though none of the Duke's restaurants are formal). The age range is from college grads to mid-thirties—the young professional crowd. The chowder houses are good places to go kick back with a good friend and catch a sports event.

Duke's Fifth Avenue Fish House Bar and Grille (206) 623-2296 is located right under the 5th Avenue Theatre and attracts pre-theater diners. Theater nights are crowded, and the dress tends to be more formal. The age range depends on the theater productions, but generally thirty-five to fifty-plus. Reservations are a must on theater nights.

# Etta's Seafood

*2020 Western Avenue*
*Just north of the Pike Place Market*
*Seattle*
*(206) 443-6000*
*$$ (Market Price)*

Etta's Seafood has good food, colorful decor—and happy customers. You'll find things such as metal fish-skeleton coat hooks, teal booths, blue tiles, and framed mirrors. The noise level is moderate, so conversation is possible. Dress is casual and comfortable. The real appeal of Etta's is the food—fresh Northwest seafood, including oysters, lobster, scallops, crab and fish selections. You can also order salad, chicken or steak. All entrées are prepared with great love and care. The staff is warm and friendly, and they ensure a great meal from start to finish.

Etta's Seafood is open from 11:30 A.M. to 10:00 P.M., Monday through Thursday; 11:30 A.M. to 11:00 P.M. Friday; 9:00 A.M. to 11:00 P.M. Saturday; and 9:00 A.M. to 10:00 P.M. Sunday.

# Flo-Anna's Diner

*14707 Bothell Way NE*
*Seattle*
*(206) 367-5562*
*$$*

Flo-Anna's Diner has that "hang-out" feeling of Al's on *Happy Days*. They serve up great big, greasy meals. If you eat there once, you'll soon become a regular! Weekend mornings are very busy here. The age range is thirty and older, but the twenty-something crowd also eats here. The atmosphere is relaxed, casual, and fairly quiet.

Flo-Anna's Diner is open and serving seven days a week from 6:00 A.M. to 9:00 P.M. for your eating pleasure!

# Honey Bear Bakery

*2106 N 55th*
*Green Lake/Seattle*
*(206) 545-7296*

This all-natural baked goods and vegetarian café is the hot-spot for Saturday and Sunday breakfast in Seattle. The Honey Bear Bakery is located just up the street from Green Lake Park, and it's a great place to stop for lunch after a day of biking, roller-blading, walking or jogging around Green Lake. The atmosphere is country-casual and the service is friendly. The crowd varies in age, but is mostly mid-twenties and over. Dress is casual and comfortable. The noise level is quiet to medium, depending on the time of day and crowd. Saturday and Sunday mornings are always crowded and the locals all seem to know each other. I suggest a cinnamon bun and then a long walk around the lake!

The Honey Bear Bakery is open from 6:00 A.M. to 11:00 P.M.

# Ivar's Acres of Clams Restaurant and Seafood Bar

*Pier 54 on Alaskan Way*
*Waterfront*
*(206) 624-6852*
*$*

Located right on the water, the Fish Bar makes for a fun, casual meal for fish-and-chip lovers. It's also a good place for those who prefer clams-and-chips or oysters-and-chips. You can sit out on the deck, watch the ferries ply the Sound, and feed the seagulls. Perfect for warm summer nights. The dress is as casual as you want to make it. This place stays open until 2:00 A.M. daily and year-round, so a late dinner is always available. They accept Visa, Mastercard and personal checks. However, after 11:00 P.M., it is cash only.

Around the corner is Ivar's Acres of Clams. This indoor restaurant and lounge is a little dressier and attracts an older crowd. Typically, the age range is twenty-five and older, but during the tourist season you'll find all ages. The atmosphere is fun and relaxed. The dress is casual to nice (no cutoffs, etc.). The lounge serves appetizers and is more a place to wait for a table than a hopping bar. Ivar's has long been known to serve a great, fresh seafood dinner. There are a few non-seafood selections such as beef and chicken entrées. The restaurant is open from 11:00 A.M. to 11:00 P.M., every night during the summer; winter hours are 11:00 A.M. to 10:00 P.M. on weeknights. All major credit cards and checks are accepted.

## Ivar's Salmon House and Fish Bar

*401 NE Northlake Way*
*Wallingford/on Lake Union*
*(206) 632-7223*
*Salmon House: $$*
*Fish Bar: $*

Ivar's Indian Salmon House and Fish Bar is the location of both a nice restaurant and a fast-food bar. This makes it ideal for any kind of date or get-together. The inside of the Salmon House, which features a Northwest Native American theme, with totem poles and a hand-carved canoe, has won design awards. It's truly spectacular, and makes you feel as if you are a part of Native-American history. The house specialty is alder-smoked entrées prepared on an open fire pit. The *Seattle Weekly* voted Ivar's the "best salmon in Seattle."

With a beautiful, close-up view of Lake Union, the restaurant attracts a sophisticated and mellow crowd. Happy Hour in the lounge is on Friday from 4:00 to 6:30 P.M., and things can get fairly loud. However, after that time, you can relax and enjoy a peaceful drink. The typical age range of the crowd is forty and over. The dress is casual to nice and business attire is a very common sight at dinner. The dining room serves dinner from 4:30 to 11:00 P.M. Monday through Friday; from 4:00 to 11:00 P.M. on Saturday; and from 4:00 to 10:00 P.M. on Sunday. The Salmon House accepts Visa, Mastercard and personal checks.

The Fish Bar serves from 11:00 A.M. to 10:00 P.M. Sunday through Thursday, and 11:00 A.M. to 11:00 P.M. Friday and Saturday (until midnight on weekends in the summer). You can take your food to the waterfront deck, or have a picnic at nearby Gas Works Park. Sitting out on the deck at night, under the stars, can make for a romantic (and inexpensive) late date.

# The Keg Restaurant

*3600 128th SE*
*Factoria/Bellevue*
*(425) 644-9700*
*$$*

Keg Restaurants are great spots to go with a date or a friend. The restaurants have semi-secluded booths and tables, surrounded by dark wood. The warm and friendly service will make you feel right at home. The dress is generally casual. The food is moderately priced, so it needn't be an expensive evening. But don't let the prices fool you. The Keg serves some of the best steak and seafood around. They also have an outstanding salad bar. During the summer months, the restaurants proudly serve BIG lobsters nightly.

The lounge sections can range from quiet and uncrowded to mobbed and noisy, depending on the hour, the night and the decibel level of the music. Weekly drink specials are a feature.

The Keg Restaurants are open from 11:00 A.M. to 1:30 A.M. Monday through Friday; from 11:30 A.M. to 1:30 A.M. Saturday; and from 9:30 A.M. to 12:30 A.M. Sundays. These late hours make them a popular late-dinner spot. The typical age range is eighteen to forty, but you'll see all ages here. The Keg accepts Visa, Mastercard, American Express and personal checks. Reservations are suggested, especially on weekend nights.

The Factoria Keg is across the street from Factoria Cinemas, making "dinner and a movie" very convenient. The Kirkland Keg is perfect for an evening stroll along Lake Washington.

Other Keg Restaurant locations:
15323 Westminster Way N, Lynnwood (206) 362-5131
180 SW 148th, Burien, Seattle (206) 241-0905
2500 SW Barton, West Seattle, Seattle (206) 935-0640
10600 NE 38th Place, Kirkland (425) 822-5131
6434 Bothell Way NE, Kenmore (206) 485-5514

# Kidd Valley

*5910 Lake Washington Boulevard NE*
*Kirkland*
*(425) 827-5888*
*$*

Don't rule out Kidd Valley just because it's fast food! This is "fast" food prepared fresh daily on the premises and cooked while you watch. Kidd Valley rates the "Best Cheeseburger" and a "Favorite Place for Burgers" by *The Weekly*. The Kirkland restaurant is very new and fresh-looking, with speedy service. You can eat outside and watch the sunset over Lake Washington. Another great idea is to take your order to one of the many Kirkland beaches for a picnic. (Marsh Park is only half a block down the street.)

For those of you old enough, or native-Northwestern enough to remember, Herfy's and Kidd Valley and Dick's were the original local burger chains. Now Ivar's owns Kidd Valley, but after all, they're a home-grown chain as well.

Kidd Valley in Kirkland is open from 10:30 A.M. to 9:00 P.M. Monday through Saturday, and from 11:00 A.M. to 9:00 P.M. on Sunday.

Other Kidd Valleys (without views) are located at:
4910 Greenlake Way N, Seattle (206) 547-0121
15259 Bel-Red Road, Bellevue (425) 643-4165
6434 Bothell Way NE, Bothell (425) 485-5514
3000 184th SW, Lynnwood (425) 771-4905
135 15th E, Capitol Hill (206) 328-8133
531 Queen Anne Avenue N, Seattle (206) 284-0184

# Mamma Melina Ristorante

*4759 Roosevelt Way NE*
*University District/Seattle*
*(206) 632-2271*
*$$*

Mamma Melina's is owned and run by first-generation Italians and the ambiance is that of an Italian deli. Beautiful murals of Italy decorate the walls. The recipes are from Naples, and the food is seasoned with a balance of vegetables and spices. Delicious!

Mamma Melina's is located beneath the 7 Gables Theater and is just around the corner from the Metro Theaters. You'll find people of all ages here.

Mamma Melina's is open from 5:00 P.M. to 9:30 P.M. Monday through Thursday, from 5:00 P.M. to 10:15 P.M. Friday, from 4:30 P.M. to 10:15 P.M. Saturday, and from 4:30 P.M. to 9:30 P.M. Sunday. Make reservations, because this place is very popular and very good! Parking can be difficult, but there is a parking lot off 9th Street across from the Metro Theaters.

## Mama's Mexican Kitchen

*2234 Second Avenue (at Bell Street)*
*Downtown/Belltown area*
*(206) 728-6262*
*$*

Mama's Mexican Kitchen looks like a Southern California/Baja hole-in-the-wall. Never mind the very casual ambiance; the Southern-California style Mexican food is great! This place was possibly the first Mexican restaurant in the area (opened in 1974*), and it's been going strong ever since. The interior reminds you of a Los Angeles diner, with its vinyl booths and bright news flyers on the walls. Outdoor dining is available during the summer, right on the sidewalk. Mama's is loud and busy, like any good Mexican restaurant should be, and the beer is cold.

All of the Mexican-American favorites are on the menu, and there's even a *not hot* item called "Screamers." This was rated one of the best ethnic restaurants in Seattle and you'll see why. Plan on having a great time, but don't dress up. Personal checks and credit cards are welcome.

*The first Mama's started in Hawaii, and there are now three locations in the Islands. All, including the Seattle restaurant, are still operated by the same owner.

# McCormick & Schmick's

*1103 First Avenue*
*Downtown Seattle*
*(206) 623-5500*
*$$*

Located in the heart of downtown Seattle, McCormick and Schmick's is a lively place to take a date or to meet a friend after work. The restaurant has a casual and comfortable appeal which also makes it a nice "get-to-know-you" place. The atmosphere comes alive with the "after-work" crowd and is a "happening" late-night spot as well. Typically, the age range is from twenty-five to forty-five—the professional crowd. Dress is business attire for those coming straight from work, or casual if you have time to change.

The dining room specializes in seafood and the menu changes daily to offer fresh specials. The decor of the dining room is casual, with a lot of wood and brass. This eatery can get noisy, so don't plan an intimate getaway here. Do plan on a great meal, a lot of fun, and a busy atmosphere. Reservations are suggested, especially on weekend nights. They accept personal checks, AMEX, Mastercard, and Visa.

McCormick and Schmick's has a late-bar menu, which includes drink specials, from 11:00 P.M. to closing (which is sometime after 1:00 A.M.). Happy Hour light menu specials in the bar are a great deal, serving calamari, oyster shooters, chicken wings, mussels, burgers, fettucine, etc., and are served from 3:00 P.M. to 6:00 P.M. on weekdays, and from 5:00 to 6:00 P.M. on weekends.

Other McCormick & Schmick Restaurants to try:

The Harborside at 1200 Westlake Avenue N, Seattle (206) 270-9052. The Harborside has a great bar with tons of atmosphere. It looks over the water and has a spectacular view of the city.

The Fish House and Bar at 722 4th Avenue, Seattle (206) 682-3900. The Fish House and Bar also serves the same great food in a casual atmosphere. Some of the best fresh seafood in Seattle.

## Nikolas Pizza and Pasta

*1924 N 45th*
*Seattle*
*(206) 545-9090*
*$$*

Nikolas is famous for their omelets, and once you've tried them you'll see why! The atmosphere is very light and pleasant, almost atrium-like. This restaurant makes a great morning date on Saturday or Sunday. The typical age is mid-twenties and up, but anyone will feel right at home here. Dress is casual. For dinner, enjoy a continental menu with Greek and Italian influences. You can order just about anything, including salads, burgers, pasta and pizza.

Nikolas is open from 11:00 A.M. to 10:00 P.M. Monday through Thursday, 11:00 A.M. to 11:00 P.M. Friday, 8:00 A.M. to 11:00 P.M. Saturday, and 8:00 A.M. to 10:00 P.M. Sunday.

## Northlake Tavern

*660 NE Northlake Way*
*University District/Lake Union*
*(206) 633-5317 ("to go" phone)*
*$-$$*

*(Note: The Northlake Tavern is a tavern, and a valid ID is required.)*

The Northlake Tavern serves Seattle's heftiest pizza and provides a fun and lively atmosphere for a casual dinner date. The brightly painted walls display cartoons of UW characters and pizza jokes. The typical age range is from twenty-one to sixty-plus, with the majority current or past students at the UW. or boaters from the nearby marinas. Be prepared for a loud and always crowded dining experience. The tables and booths are fairly close together, so there isn't a lot of privacy, but the Northlake provides a casual and relaxed atmosphere, plus that legendary pizza that has kept lines forming since 1952. There are "classic Italian" entrées as well, but most everyone comes for the pizza. Be prepared to put your name on the list, and wait up to 45 minutes or more, especially on weekend nights. "Take-out" pizza is yet another option, but call first! Gas Works Park, which is just down the street, makes a great place for a "pizza picnic."

The Northlake's hours are from 1:00 to 11:00 P.M. on Sunday; from 11:00 A.M. to 12:00 noon on Monday through Thursday, and from 11:00 P.M. to 1:00 A.M. on Friday and Saturday. The pizza price depends on what you put on it. The Northlake Tavern accepts Visa and Mastercard, but no personal checks.

# Ponti Seafood Grille

*3014 Third N*
*North Queen Anne/Near Fremont Bridge*
*Seattle*
*(206) 284-3000*
*$$*

The atmosphere alone is reason enough to visit Ponti. Located right on the channel leading to Lake Union and directly in view of the Fremont Bridge, this seafood grille is a great escape. Lunch or Sunday brunch are excellent options. The boating activity in the narrow channel below will remind you of the canal scene in Amsterdam, and the Fremont bridge raises now and again for drama. In nice weather, you can enjoy the early evening with a drink and appetizer outside on either the deck or patio.

For dinner, the white linen tablecloths and dim lights set a romantic mood. Ponti is a quiet, upscale setting. The bar is smallish, but very lively at night. There is a big fireplace at one end, adding a cozy touch during the winter months. The age ranges from twenty-five to forty-ish, and the dress is "well put-together." If you are simply enjoying the outside deck, then casual, but not unkempt, dress is appropriate.

Dinner is served from 5:30 P.M. to 10:00 P.M., Sunday through Thursday and from 5:30 P.M. to 11:00 P.M., Friday and Saturday. The Bar is open until 1:00 A.M. on weeknights and until 2:00 A.M. on weekends. Ponti suggests reservations.

# Red Robin Gourmet Burgers & Spirits

*Eastlake E & Fuhrman E*
*University District (south of the bridge)*
*Seattle*
*(206) 323-0917*
*$-$$*

Located up on the bluff overlooking Portage Bay, the "original" Red Robin has been a popular casual date destination since 1943. From humble origins as the closest tavern to the campus, this Red Robin hatched a full-fledged franchise operation. The tavern-now-restaurant is decorated with bright colors and plants, and the menu is extensive.

The house specialty is off-beat burgers and wacky drinks. Your companion may or may not be impressed by someone who orders a Rookie Magic or Later Alligator, or the all-time favorite, Flat on Your Beak. The bar has tables which sit beneath greenhouse windows, overlooking the water, and there is outdoor seating on the deck. You can watch the boats below, and maybe see the University Bridge open for the big yachts. Happy Hour is from 3:00 P.M. to 6:00 P.M. and 10:00 P.M. to closing, and it can get pretty loud during this time.

The age range is from eighteen to thirty-something on weekend nights (UW students make up the majority) and a little older during the week. The hours are from 11:00 A.M. to 11:00 P.M. Monday through Thursday; from 11:00 A.M. to 1:00 A.M. Friday and Saturday; and from 11:00 A.M. to 11:00 P.M. Sunday. The Red Robin does not take reservations. Visa, Mastercard and AMEX are all taken, but no personal checks.

Other locations:
Downtown: 1100 4th, Seattle (206) 447-1909
Overlake: 2390 148th NE, Redmond (425) 641-3810
Pier 55: 1101 Alaskan Way, Seattle (206) 623-1942

# The Roost

*120 NW Gilman Boulevard*
*Issaquah*
*(423) 392-5550*
*$$*

The Roost (related to the Mick McHugh restaurants such as The Roaster in Kirkland) is named after Issaquah's first business establishment, a saloon. At that time (1887), Issaquah was called Squak. Today's Roost is both restaurant and lounge. The dress, like the atmosphere, is casual and relaxed, and the meals are inexpensive. Issaquah has progressed well beyond its humble beginnings, but is still a little town which you and your companion might want to explore together. There are country roads, lots of hiking and biking opportunities not far away, and the ski slopes 45 minutes east. It's easy to make a day of it and end up at the Roost. The noise level is medium to quiet, except in the bar. The typical age range is about twenty-five and up—older than college age.

The bar is a fun place to have a drink, with a Happy Hour from 3:00 to 8:00 P.M. Monday through Friday. Dinner is served until 9:00 P.M. Monday through Thursday, and until 10:00 P.M. on Saturday and Sunday. They accept major credit cards and personal checks. Reservations are recommended.

# Shiro's Sushi

*2401 Second Avenue*
*Seattle*
*(206) 443-9844*
*$$*

Shiro's Sushi was opened by sushi chef Shiro Kashiba (creator of Nikko) in Seattle's Belltown District. The restaurant is small and intimate, serving sushi and teriyaki dishes, both with rice and soup. The casual atmosphere is friendly and relaxed. This place is a "must" for anyone who loves sushi! Located in the newly renovated Belltown, you are just walking distance from the Belltown Pub and Belltown Billiards. Have a sushi dinner and then walk to

Belltown Billiards for a game of pool. Or, go to the Belltown Pub for a drink (located at 2322 First Avenue).

Shiro's serves dinner from 5:30 P.M. to 10:00 P.M. Monday through Saturday and is closed on Sunday.

## Shoo Be Doo Diner

*11 Roy Street*
*Lower Queen Anne/Seattle*
*(206) 378-0520*
*$*

Good golly, Miss Molly! The '50s lends inspiration to this bright friendly diner within walking distance of the Seattle Center. A neon Elvis does a "whole lot of shakin'" while you play jukebox oldies from the Seeburg Wall-O-Matic in your booth. Framed photos of movie stars from Our Gang and the Lone Ranger to Marilyn Monroe and James Dean complement the gourmet burgers, huge sandwiches, and jumbo dogs. Burgers, which come with a generous side of fries, can be ordered as singles or doubles; the daily special usually includes hearty fare such as beef roast or meat loaf. For lighter meals, choose from several soup and salad offerings. Soft drinks, shakes, ice cream specialties, beer, and wine round out the menu. It's a perfect stop before a Sonics game or a Key Arena concert. The diner is popular with those in the twenty to forty age range, but you'll find the older crowd there, too. Dress is casual, as you'd expect.

Shoo Be Doo Diner is open from 11:00 A.M. to 10:00 P.M. Sunday through Thursday; Friday and Saturday they stay open until 11:00 P.M. Breakfast is served Saturday and Sunday from 8:00 A.M. to noon. All major credit cards and personal checks are accepted, with proper identification.

## Stella's Trattoria

*4500 Ninth NE*
*University District*
*(206) 633-1100*
*$-$$*

Stella's Trattoria is a warm and friendly restaurant with good Italian food. Open 24 hours a day, it's also an ideal late-night spot (See *Movie Theaters*, chapter 7). You can see a movie at the Metro cineplex upstairs, then come down to Stella's for a midnight snack. The dinner menu is served from 4:00 P.M. until 11:00 P.M., then a late night menu is available, which is a mix of dinner and breakfast options. The atmosphere is casual and very comfortable. The walls are covered with art and posters, and there are plants all around. The little wood tables and high walls give Stella's the feeling of an outdoor café. The age ranges from twenty-one to fifty-plus, depending on the hour. Stella's accepts all major credit cards and personal checks.

## T.G.I. Fridays

*505 Park Place*
*Park Place Shopping Center*
*Downtown Kirkland*
*(425) 828-3743*
*$*

T.G.I. Fridays is a great place for a fun evening no matter any night of the week. This is an ideal place to bring a first date, simply because there is so much activity, it's easy to join in. If you are with a longtime love, you may find this place a little on the loud side, but you can always sit closer together.

There are lots of appetizers and exotic drinks, and the menu has something for everyone; choose from salads, burgers, steaks, chicken, pasta and fajitas (to name only a few of the selections). Dress is casual, but not grubby. Typically, the age range is from twenty-one to fifty-plus on the weekends, and from thirty and older weeknights. Outdoor seating is available when weather permits.

T.G.I. Fridays is open until midnight Monday through Thursday, until 2:00 A.M. Friday and Saturday, and until 1:00 A.M. on Sundays. These late hours make it perfect to stop in after a movie, especially since the Kirkland Parkplace Cineplex (see page 141) is right next door. You can make it dinner and a movie, without moving your car. T.G.I. Fridays accepts all major credit cards, but no personal checks.

Another great location to try is at 1001 Fairview Avenue N, Seattle (206) 621-7290. This T.G.I. Fridays sits right on Lake Union and has a great view of the Seattle skyline. The great service and delicious food is the same at both restaurants.

## Yarrow Bay Beach Cafe

*1270 Carillon Point*
*Kirkland*
*(425) 889-9052*
*$-$$*

Located below the Yarrow Bay Grille, the Beach Cafe is more casual, and the accent is on noisy fun. The atmosphere is lively, with bright colors and flags adding a nautical touch. When weather permits, outdoor seating is available on the deck. This is a good place to kick back and unwind at the edge of Lake Washington. The age range is from twenty to forty, but both younger and older will feel comfortable eating here.

The bar is lively and attracts a crowd ranging from twenty-one to thirty-ish. Dinner is served from 5:00 to 10:00 P.M. Sunday through Thursday, and from 5:00 to 11:00 P.M. Friday and Saturday. The bar is open from 11:00 A.M. to 12:00 A.M. Sunday through Thursday, and from 11:00 to 1:30 A.M. Friday and Saturday. Reservations are suggested, depending on the weather.

# LOUD & LIVELY RESTAURANTS

## Azteca Restaurants

*See locations below*
*$-$$*

Good Mexican food, relatively inexpensive, is the hallmark of this popular local chain of restaurants and lounges. (Still family-owned after 20 years in the northwest, and still dedicated to authentic recipes and "amigos"-style hospitality.) The interiors vary, but the general idea is to look like a Mexican Cantina. There are 26 Azteca's in the Seattle area, and each caters to the neighborhood clientele. Some have strolling Mariachis; some are more family-oriented than others.

The Shilshole and Lake Union restaurants are right on the water, and are popular with couples, as are the other Azteca locations. You can expect the noise level to be quiet enough to carry on a conversation, but loud enough to keep things lively. The dress is casual and the age range varies greatly, although the bars do seem to cater to the thirty-plus crowd.

The lounges are comfortable and have a full menu of their own. Entertainment varies from site to site Look for Karaoke at some of the lounges. Impress your date by singing his/her favorite song. If you don't want to sing, just laugh at everyone who does.

The restaurants keep individual hours, but generally serve from 11:00 A.M. to 10:30 P.M. during the week and from 11:00 A.M. to 11:30 P.M. on the weekends. They accept all major credit cards and personal checks.

Bellevue:      150 112th Avenue NE
               Bellevue
               (425) 453-9087

               3040 148th NE
               Overlake
               (425) 881-8700

Lake Union:    2501 Fairview E
               (206) 324-4941

| Shilshole: | 6017 Seaview NW |
| | (206) 789-7373 |
| South Center: | 17555 Southcenter Parkway |
| | (206) 575-0990 |

## Beppo Little Italy

*701 Ninth Avenue N*
*Seattle*
*(206) 244-2288*
*$$*

You know Beppo Little Italy is a fun place just by looking at their business cards which read: "CALL AHEAD INSTEAD—DIAL BIG-A-BUT." That kind of fun atmosphere is what you will find inside the restaurant. The decor is Italian, and the walls covered with humorous Italian photographs. The oversized menu is mounted on the wall. The delicious entrées are "family-size"— huge portions—and feature southern Italian food. The portions are so big, the waiters bring you shopping bags to take your leftovers home. If you like pizza, I suggest the two-foot-long pizza. The noise level is loud and the dress is casual. You will find all ages eating here, from six to sixty! It's an ideal dinner spot for friends, families and dates.

Beppo starts serving at 5:00 P.M. Monday through Friday, at 4:30 P.M. Saturday, and at 4:00 P.M. on Sunday. Dinner is over when everyone goes home! Make sure you call ahead for reservations; otherwise expect a very long wait. There are limited reservations, so make your plans early!

## Black Angus

*1411 156th NE*
*Crossroads Area/Bellevue*
*(425) 746-1663*
*$-$$*

The Black Angus chain serves very good food at very good prices. The high booths and dark lighting make the restaurant a romantic and intimate spot, yet the dress is casual. The menu offers mainly steak and seafood, but chicken and other items are available. The servings are generous and the price is reasonable. Reservations are strongly suggested for weekend nights. Credit cards and personal checks are accepted.

The bar at the Bellevue location has a country theme (Black Angus Square Cow Fun Bar) and really jumps at night. The bar has dancing and plays Top 40 music. It is a great place to dance the night away. The average age is the older college graduate, twenty-five to thirty, but the forty to fifty-plus crowd is commonplace.

Other Locations:
Burien: 15820 1st (206) 244-5700
Everett: 8413 Evergreen Way (425) 355-7400

## Broadway New American Grille

*314 Broadway E*
*Seattle*
*(206) 328-7000*
*$*

Perfect for late night diners, the Broadway New American Grille serves a full menu until 1:00 A.M. on weekend nights. The glass roof and big windows give the restaurant a light, airy atmosphere. Menu options include burgers, salads, pastas. The noise level can range from medium to loud, depending on the night and crowd. The emphasis here is on having fun and eating good food with good friends. The age range is from twenty-one to thirty-five-ish, and there is an adjoining bar. The hours are from 11:00 A.M. to 2:00 A.M. Monday through Friday and from 10:00 A.M. to 2:00 A.M. on Saturday and Sunday. No reservations are necessary. Visa, Mastercard, AMEX and personal checks accepted.

## Cucina! Cucina!

*901 Fairview Avenue N*
*Seattle*
*(206) 447-2782*
*$$*

Cucina! Cucina! Italian Cafe is one of the liveliest spots in Seattle. Located right on Lake Union, this restaurant serves up beautifully prepared Italian dishes. The pasta dishes are absolutely delicious. The service is always excellent and the atmosphere is light and casual. At night it can get very noisy, especially if you are near the bar. During the summer you can dine outside, under the stars (heat lamps are provided for those cool Seattle nights) and watch the moon over Lake Union. The restaurant crowd is generally twenty-one and older, but families are also a common sight.

Cucina! Cucina! at Carillon Point (2220 Carillon Point, Kirkland (425) 822-4000) has a stunning view overlooking Lake Washington. Once again, it has the same wonderful food, atmosphere and service as the Seattle location.

Cucina! Cucina! in Bellevue Place (800 Bellevue Way, (425) 637-1177) has the same great food and atmosphere, but without the view. Located conveniently in Downtown Bellevue, it is a great pre-or post-movie spot.

Cucina! Presto! is a great extension of the popular Cucina! Cucina! and can be found all over the Seattle area. This mini-Cucina! offers a casual alternative, with great tasting takeout.

Look for Cucina! Presto! at:

Crossroads: 1299 156th Avenue NE (425) 562-4646
Elliott Avenue: 1144 Elliott Avenue W (206) 217-0200
Factoria: 3615 128th Avenue SE (425) 747-3000
Kirkland: 92 Central Way (425) 739-9344
Mercer Island: 7807 SE 27th Street (206) 236-6888
Queen Anne: 2128 Queen Anne Avenue N (206) 217-9900

# Da Vinci's

*89 Kirkland Avenue*
*Downtown Kirkland*
*(425) 889-9000*
*$-$$*

Couples love the boisterous atmosphere of Da Vinci's as much as the food. The house specialties are pizza, pasta and cocktails. This place looks like something right out of New York City. The walls are covered with graffiti and posters. The bar opens up onto Kirkland's main street, affording terrific people-watching opportunities. The restaurant also has outdoor seating on the side street. The age range varies with the season and the night. During the summer, you'll find more college kids, home for summer vacation. The school year draws an older crowd, and the locals. Generally, the age range is twenty-one to forty-plus. Whatever your age, if you like to have fun, you'll love Da Vinci's. Wednesdays and Thursdays feature Karaoke in the bar, and on Fridays and Saturdays in the restaurant. The restaurant is open from 11:30 A.M. to 1:00 A.M. (ish!). The bar hours vary, depending on the crowd. Da Vinci's accepts Mastercard, Visa, American Express and personal checks.

# Deluxe Bar and Grille

*625 Broadway E*
*Seattle*
*(206) 324-9697*
*$*

The Deluxe is one of Broadway's oldest hangouts (opened in 1962), and continues to serve some of the best burgers in town. It also makes a perfect first date, or spot to hit for a nightcap after a movie or play. The establishment is small and comfortable, with some outdoor seating. It is a great place to hang out in jeans and a tee-shirt and get to know each other. They don't take reservations, so it's first come, first served. The music is medium-to-loud, and there is always conversation noise. The crowd ranges from twenty-one to thirty-five-ish and tends to be very lively. The hours are from 11:00 A.M. to 2:00 A.M. Monday through Friday, and from 10:00 A.M. to 2:00 A.M. on Saturday and Sunday.

## The Duchess Tavern

*2728 NE 55th*
*University Village area*
*(206) 527-8606*
*21 and older, identification required*
*$*

The Duchess—Juke Joint, Sports Bar and Eatery—is perfect for all you sports lovers out there. Established in 1934, this tav is very popular with UW students, especially the "Greeks." But don't let this scare you away! The Duchess is also an "after-game" hangout for many of the local business-sponsored sports teams around Seattle. Typically, the crowd is twenty-one to forty-plus. The Duchess has television sets all around the bar, pool tables and dart boards.

Dress is casual, and the atmosphere is medium-to-loud. Definitely a spot for a casual evening, the Duchess doesn't offer intimate surroundings. The menu includes appetizers and burgers, and the bar serves beer by the pitcher. Things get even more active during the Husky football season. In fact, the Duchess opens early on Husky game days (8:30 A.M.). The regular hours are from 4:00 P.M. to 2:00 A.M. Monday through Friday; 11:00 A.M. to 2:00 A.M. Saturday; and 11:00 A.M. to 12:00 A.M. Sunday.

## Kells Irish Restaurant and Pub

*1916 Post Alley*
*Pike Place Market*
*(206) 728-1916*
*$-$$*

Kells, tucked away on Post Alley, is a traditional Irish pub, decorated in the traditional Irish manner. This translates into dark wood, dim light and a warm ambiance. The walls are covered with paintings and photographs of Ireland. The menu features traditional Irish meals, including Hibernian Salads, Dublin Coddle, Irish Stew and Ethna's Irish Breads (to name a few).

The adjoining bar is an authentic Irish pub, with good ol' Irish beers. Irish music is always playing, but there is also live Irish music and dancing on certain evenings. The bar hosts live music Wednesday through Saturday, starting at 9:00 P.M. Dress is casual and the atmosphere relaxed. Everyone from any age range is welcome at Kells, twenty-one and up in the pub. Kells has its regulars, who are in the thirty-plus range, but on weekend nights, college students occupy the pub as well.

Outdoor seating is available during the summer months, which adds to the overall European flavor. Dinner is served until 9:30 P.M., Monday through Thursday and Sunday, and until 10:00 P.M. Friday and Saturday. Reservations are strongly recommended for Friday and Saturday nights. When asked what time the pub closed, the Irish hostess replied, "When everyone gets tired!" Kells accepts Visa, Mastercard and local checks.

## La Cocina and Cantina

*432 Broadway E*
*Seattle*
*(206) 323-1676*
*$*

How about Mexican food, or maybe just a Margarita at La Cocina and Cantina? The restaurant opens up onto the street when the weather is nice. The inside is decorated like an authentic Mexican Cantina and is always hopping with activity. All ages feel right at home here, and the atmosphere is pure fun. The food is authentic and reasonably priced. The hours are from 11:00 A.M. to 12:00 A.M. Monday through Thursday, from 11:00 A.M. to 1:00 A.M. Friday, from 11:30 A.M. to 1:00 A.M. Saturday, and from 11:30 A.M. to 11:00 P.M. Sunday. La Cocina and Cantina accepts credit cards, but no personal checks. No reservations are needed.

## La Cocina del Puerco

*10246 Main Street*
*Old Bellevue*
*(425) 455-1151*
*$*

Truly authentic Mexican food is unusual in the Northwest, but you can find it at La Cocina del Puerco, located in Old Bellevue. Don't expect the usual nachos and burritos, however.

The food is served cafeteria-style, and is very mild, unless you load on the hot salsa and jalapeños. The atmosphere is funky, cantina-Mexican, with piñatas and Mexican signs hanging from ceiling and walls, and authentic metal tables and chairs. There are tables outside, much like in Mexico and Spain. Inside, the tables are fairly close together; although it isn't very private, it's friendly. The Mexican music can be loud—add a full house and it's not a quiet place! In warm weather, you can sit outside and watch the foot and automobile traffic on Main Street, while enjoying a cool drink and hot dinner. After dinner, take a stroll along Old Main Street and do a little window-shopping. Dress is as casual as the surroundings, and the age range is typically from twenty-five to fifty-plus.

La Cocina del Puerco is open from 11:30 A.M. to 9:00 P.M., Monday through Thursday; from 11:30 A.M. to 10:00 P.M., Friday and Saturday; and from 1:00 P.M. to 9:00 P.M. on Sunday. No reservations are taken, and on busy nights you'll search for a table. They accept major credit cards, but no personal checks.

# Latitude 47

*1232 Westlake Avenue N*
*West Lake Union*
*(206) 284-1047*
*$$*

The decor and location of Latitude 47 make you think nautical. The giant windows give you the sensation that you can almost reach out and touch Lake Union. Bamboo chairs and plants create the exotic flavor of a sea-side paradise. A candlelit table for two, right on the water's edge, awaits you. The specialty is seafood, and the restaurant's claim to fame is having "Seattle's Freshest Seafood." The dress leans towards dressy, and the typical age range is twenty-one to thirty-something. The restaurant serves dinner from 5:00 P.M. to 9:30 P.M. weeknights, and from 5:00 P.M. to 10:00 P.M. on the weekends.

Latitude 47 also has a hopping lounge, called Club 47. Here you can enjoy videos, dancing and large-screen sports viewing. Club 47 is open until 2:00 A.M. and is a great place to dance the night away. The dress tends to be more casual than the restaurant, but no shorts allowed. There is a $3.00 cover and Karaoke is featured every Thursday night from 7:30 to 10:30 P.M. On

Wednesdays and Sundays you can try Latin dancing from 9:00 P.M. to 1:30 A.M. Lambada!

Reservations are suggested, especially on weekends. They accept major credit cards and personal checks.

## Lox, Stock and Bagel

*4552 University Way N*
*University District*
*(206) 634-3144*
*21 and older (valid identification required)*
*$*

A true UW gathering spot, the Lox, Stock and Bagel is a fun and inexpensive, place to spend an evening. The atmosphere is casual, with palm trees and bright pictures decorate the walls. The menu has something for everyone, from ethnic to burgers and salads. Typically, the clientele is twenty-one to thirty; depending on the night, the crowd can be older. Music nights are Wednesday, Friday and Saturday, and the cover is only $2.00 Fridays and Saturdays (Wednesday is free). These nights attract the most couples and the greatest age range, depending on the group playing. Lox, Stock and Bagel claims to have the cheapest music in town. You and your companion can enjoy an evening of great music, and still have enough money left to enjoy the food and drink. The music is typically loud, so don't anticipate a quiet, romantic atmosphere. However, do expect lots of noisy fun. Lox, Stock and Bagel is open until 2:00 A.M. every night and accepts Visa, Mastercard, and personal checks with the proper ID.

## Planet Hollywood

*1500 Sixth Avenue*
*Downtown Seattle*
*(206) 287-0001*
*$$*

Inspired by the glamour of Hollywood and owned by superstars such as Bruce Willis, Demi Moore, Sylvester Stallone and Arnold Schwarzenegger, Planet Hollywood is a wild place for dinner. The Seattle location joins the ranks of cities such as Los Angeles and

San Francisco. The restaurant is filled with movie memorabilia from floor to ceiling. This makes a great first date spot because if you don't have anything to say to each other, you can talk about all the movie "stuff" around you. There is always loud music playing, TV screens flashing, and people talking. The tables are fairly close together, so don't expect an intimate dinner for two. The food is good and the menu has fun names for the salads, sandwiches and burgers. Be sure to check out the souvenir shop before heading out the door; you might find a nice gift for your date.

Planet Hollywood is open every day from 11:00 A.M. to 1:00 A.M. (that's seven days a week)! It is a lot of fun for a late-night date, after a movie, or after a busy day of shopping. Planet Hollywood accepts all major credit cards and cash only.

## Ram Cafe and Sports Bar

*4730 University Village*
*University District*
*(206) 525-3565*
*$-$$*

For those who love sports, Ram's is a great place. The walls are covered with sports photos and the atmosphere is as boisterous as cheering for the home team. TVs in every room broadcast sporting events all day and all night. This is "the" place to watch Seattle home teams play! Make sure you go early, because the place is always packed. The food is great and the menu offers a wide variety of entrées. Close to the University of Washington, the college crowd makes up the majority of the customers. However, there is a regular crowd which ranges from thirty and up, so it's not just a college party.

The adjoining bar always hops and serves the full menu as well. Happy Hour runs from 3:00 to 6:00 P.M. and from 10:00 P.M. to 1:30 A.M. Karaoke is a big hit Tuesdays and Saturdays, from 9:30 P.M. to 1:30 A.M. The restaurant's noise level is moderate-to-loud, depending on the night (weekends are louder). The bar can get louder yet, especially with the Karaoke.

Dinner is served until midnight Monday through Saturday, and until 11:00 P.M. on Sunday. The bar is open until 2:00 A.M.

*daily*. This late-night dinner service makes Ram's a great place to go after a movie or sporting event. They accept all major credit cards and personal checks.

# Roanoke Park Place Tavern

*2409 Tenth E*
*Capitol Hill*
*(206) 324-5882*
*21 and older (valid identification required)*
*$*

If you're looking for a nice, but fun, bar to just kick back and have a beer with a date or a good friend, the Roanoke Tavern is an excellent choice. The atmosphere is casual and it does, indeed, look like a bar. However, this tavern is popular with locals who strive to keep their neighborhood hangout a safe place. The Roanoke attracts college students, as well as the neighbors and sports teams. This mix adds to the tavern flavor.

The menu features burger and snack items, served until 10:00 P.M. The bar itself is open every day from 12:00 noon to 2:00 A.M. The age range is from twenty-one to forty-and-up; typically the college group shows up later, after 9:00 P.M. They accept credit cards and personal checks, with the proper ID.

## ROMANTIC RESTAURANTS

## Adriatica Restaurant

*1107 Dexter N*
*Queen Anne*
*Seattle*
*(206) 285-5000*
*$$*

White linen tablecloths and little table lamps, soft background music, outstanding service, and excellent food make Adriatica one of the most popular restaurants with couples in search of a special evening out. There are several small, cozy dining areas here. The understated interior means that you focus on each other, the view, and the food. Adriatica opened in 1977, and has received various awards including: "Best Ethnic," "Best of the Northwest," and "One of America's Top Tables."

The mood runs from casual to romantic, but dress is generally on the professional to dressy side. Dinner is served seven nights a week, from 5:30 P.M. to 10:00 P.M. Sunday through Thursday, and from 5:30 to 11:00 P.M. on Friday and Saturday. Reservations are strongly suggested. Adriatica accepts major credit cards and personal checks, with proper identification.

The bar is located upstairs, and serves appetizers. Bar hours are 5:00 P.M. to 1:00 A.M., nightly. This is an ideal late-night option after a movie or an event at Seattle Center.

## Assaggio

*2010 Fourth Avenue*
*The Claremont Hotel*
*Seattle*
*(206) 441-1399*
*$$*

Assaggio's ambiance and decor is as romantic as they come. The beautiful vaulted ceilings and walls are painted with murals that make you feel as if you're in Rome. The soft lighting, painted archways, and soft-colored carpet, walls and linen all add to the beauty of the restaurant. During the warm summer months, you can dine outside on the patio. The patio has the flavor of a European sidewalk café, with hanging vines and flowers all around. While the surroundings are romantic, the attire and mood is casual. The noise level is moderate to loud (on weekends, loud), but you can still have an intimate conversation. A variety of Italian specialties are offered, including some delicious antipasto selections. The friendly waitstaff, good food and superb wine list make Assaggio a must as a dating spot.

Assaggio serves dinner from 5:00 P.M. to 10:00 P.M. Monday through Thursday and from 5:00 P.M. to 10:30 P.M. Friday and Saturday. Voted "Best Italian Restaurant" by *Seattle Weekly*, this popular restaurant recommends reservations.

## Azaleas Fountain Court

*22 103rd NE*
*(Just off Old Bellevue Main Street)*
*Bellevue*
*(425) 451-0426*
*$$$*

Azaleas Fountain Court is one of Downtown Bellevue's best-kept romantic hideaway secrets. This elegant restaurant is tucked away in a remodeled home. Linen tablecloths, candles, the fireplace, and large French doors opening to the yard give this restaurant a cozy, homey atmosphere. The patio is secluded and perfect for intimate dining, and even these outdoor tables have formal white linen and candles. You'll feel as if you're dining on your own patio in a European villa. Dress is nice to dressy and the age range is thirty-plus. The food is a mixed menu of pasta, seafood, chicken, duck, and other mouth-watering entrées. The menu changes quarterly.

Azaleas serves dinner from 5:00 P.M. to 10:00 P.M. every night, but is closed Sunday. Reservations are a must for dinner, especially if you want to sit outside on the patio.

# Bistro Provençal

*Kirkland*
*(425) 827-3300*
*$$$*

If your idea of romance is dinner in Paris but your wallet can't quite swing it, try The Bistro Provençal. This Kirkland restaurant is as French as you can get. Blue-and-white checkered tablecloths, a brick fireplace, crisp white napkins, candles, wood beams, and the wine bottles displayed give this restaurant the ambiance of a French café. The entrées are fine French cuisine with delicacies such as "Margret de Canard aux Mures" (Duck with Boysenberries). Voted "Best French Restaurant" by *Eastside Magazine's* Reader's Poll. You can't afford to miss this bistro!

Parking along Central Way can be a challenge, but there are two parking lots on the corner of Central Way and Lake Washington Boulevard for your convenience.

# Cafe Sophie

*1921 First Avenue*
*Downtown Seattle*
*(206) 441-6139*
*$$*

"Charming" is the first word which comes to mind when describing this restaurant decorated in dark green draperies. Private little alcoves are available for intimacy. Each table has it's own little light that mimics candlelight and the glowing fireplace. Weather permitting, outdoor seating is available on the sidewalk patio. The crowd varies, as does the dress. During "prom season," this restaurant is popular with young couples in formal wear. However, the casually-dressed will not feel out of place. The patrons are a little older due to the price and sophisticated atmosphere. The nouveau cuisine is Contemporary European, and includes a variety of entrées such as chicken, fish, pasta and salads. Ask for a table in the Library, with a view of Puget Sound.

Dinner is served from 4:00 P.M. to 11:00 P.M. Sunday through Thursday, and from 4:00 P.M. to 12:00 midnight Friday and

Saturday. Cocktails are served until 2:00 A.M. and you can listen to live jazz Friday and Saturday nights. Reservations are strongly suggested on weekend nights. Cafe Sophie gladly accepts local personal checks and major credit cards.

# Campagne

*86 Pine Street*
*Pike Place Market*
*(206) 728-2800*
*$$*

Campagne is a totally enchanting restaurant. It is romantic enough to celebrate a special occasion, and quaint enough for a cozy get-to-know-each-other. Located in the Inn at the Market, the outdoor Courtyard dining area sits in the middle of the brick and ivy building. A quiet fountain gives the Courtyard an extra touch of romance. Indoors, the decor is wood and linen and *très* French. Dress tends towards dressy; sometimes tourists are more casual than locals. The noise and music level is quiet enough to allow for an intimate conversation. The food is Provincial French made with fresh Northwest ingredients, and the menu varies so that everyone can find something to suit his/her taste.

Right below Campagne, you'll find Cafe Campagne. Cafe Campagne is less formal than its upstairs cousin and less expensive too. However, you will find the same great French-style fare. Call (206) 728-CAFE for more information.

Dinner is served from 5:30 to 10:00 P.M. and the Courtyard and bar are open until 2:00 A.M. A "late night" menu is offered in both the Courtyard and bar. Reservations are a must on weekend nights. The typical age range is thirty and over, although anyone who loves romance will love this place. Campagne accepts all credit cards, but no personal checks.

# Chez Shea

*94 Pike Suite #34*
*Pike Place Market*
*Seattle*
*(206) 467-9990*
*$$$-$$$$*

Chez Shea is a small restaurant with an intimate atmosphere. All tables have a view of Puget Sound and West Seattle. If you're lucky enough to sit at a window table, you can also watch all the goings-on at the Pike Place Market below. The decor of the restaurant includes arched windows, dark wood floors, and high ceilings. The menu includes French and regional cuisine served in a creative and artistic manner. A four-course meal, with a fixed price, changes seasonally and includes salads, seafood, meats, desserts, etc. Á la carte is served Tuesday through Thursday and Sunday.

Shea's Lounge, next door, has the same great view as the restaurant and serves light meals and cocktails. . It's a great place for a late-night date after the theater.

Chez Shea is open 5:30 P.M. to 10:00 P.M. Tuesday through Sunday. The lounge is open 4:30 P.M. to midnight, Tuesday through Sunday. Chez Shea was voted "One of the Top American Restaurants" by Zagat Pacific Northwest Restaurant Survey. Reservations are suggested.

# Dilettante Chocolates

*416 Broadway E*
*Seattle*
*(206) 329-6463*
*$*

Does the name spark your interest? If so, then you'll love what's inside. Dilettante Chocolates is a combination chocolate store, espresso bar and café. At night, the restaurant is lit by candles at every table, and the setting is very romantic, but still casual. You can sip espresso and share a hot fudge sundae, while engaging in serious intellectual debate or gazing quietly into each other's eyes. And we all know that chocolate is touted as an aphrodisiac, so indulge your urge to splurge! There are no reservations, and you may have to wait for a table, especially on weekend nights. The age range is typically twenty-five and older, but pre-twenty-one couples also frequent this place. Dilettante is open from 10:00 A.M. to midnight on weekdays and until 1:00 A.M. on weekends. They accept major credit cards and personal checks.

Cafe Dilettante is located at 1600 Post Alley, near the Pike Place Market (206) 728-9144 and has marble tabletops, surrounded by glass display cases with enticing chocolates inside. It is more casual and less romantic than the Broadway location, but the treats are just as delicious!

# Eques

*900 Bellevue Way NE*
*(Hyatt Regency Hotel)*
*Downtown Bellevue*
*(425) 462-1234*
*$$*

Tucked away inside the Hyatt Regency Hotel, Eques provides a romantic and elegant Old-World setting. The tables are well-spaced (and beautifully draped), to allow for private conversations. The lights are dim, and the music is unobtrusive and soothing. The typical age range is thirty-five to forty-five, with the exception of senior proms. The clientele appears well-to-do, as befits the restaurant's atmosphere, but Eques is a great place to enjoy a nice, but not bankrupting, dinner.

Dress is usually dressy, with a few diners in casual-nice outfits. The service is always friendly, and the food is very good. The giant scallops and prawns are favorites of many customers. Valet parking is available (validated with your meal) at the Hyatt, and there is also validated self-park underneath the hotel complex.

Reservations are suggested. Major credit cards are accepted. Eques serves from 6:30 A.M. to 10:30 P.M., seven days a week.

Eques has a very appealing lounge area adjacent to the restaurant. As contrasted to the soft tones of the dining room, the bar surfaces are more angular, with wood the predominant feature. It's an ideal passage from the day's business into the evening's pleasures. Bar hours are from 4 P.M. until midnight or later (depending on the crowd).

## Fortnum's European Cafe

*10213 Main Street*
*Old Bellevue*
*(425) 455-2033*
*$-$$*

Fortnum's has been a favorite of Eastsiders for over 16 years. Whether you're here for coffee and pastries or a quiet dinner, the quality never varies. The decor is pink, with lots of paintings on the walls, and the mood is continental. The age range tends to be thirty to forty, and the daytime clientele consists of friends and business associates. Couples are a more common sight at night. Friday evenings are especially popular, since this is a great place to slow the pace and enjoy a leisurely, cozy meal. Fortnum's specializes in offering a new selection of Northwest wines every week—all good wines and all priced from $10-$20 per bottle. You can order coffee, tea, wine, beer, or champagne. You can also indulge in any kind of espresso imaginable, and the desserts are to die for!

During the nicer months, you can sit outside and enjoy the flavor of Old Main Street. But when it's nasty outside, you can enjoy a pleasant afternoon or evening inside, sipping hot coffee and talking.

Fortnum's serves breakfast from 9:00 A.M. to 11:00 A.M., Monday through Saturday, lunch from 11:00 A.M. to 3:30 P.M., Monday through Saturday, and dinner from 5:00 P.M. to 8:30 P.M., Friday. They do not take reservations, so you may have to wait for a table. Fortnum's accepts all major credit cards and personal checks.

## The Garden Court

*Four Seasons Olympic Hotel*
*411 University Street*
*Downtown Seattle*
*(206) 621-1700*
*$$*

Located in the elegant Four Seasons Hotel, the Garden Court looks just like its name. The windows reach all the way to the vaulted ceiling and there are plants everywhere. The trees are decorated with little white lights, adding a romantic touch. Trees next to a waterfall add to the tranquil ambiance. Dinner is served until 11:00 P.M.

On the weekends, the Garden Court has dancing, and a jazz and swing band sets the tone for a night of fun. A late dinner and dancing is always a near-perfect date option. Dancing begins at 9:00 P.M. and ends at 1:00 A.M.; there is no cover charge, but there is a $4.00 minimum. During these hours, the age ranges from the mid-forties to the sixties, but diners are usually age thirty and up. Dress is nice to dressy, with dancing clothes popular on the weekends.

Reservations are strongly suggested. The Garden Court accepts all major credit cards, but no personal checks (hotel policy).

## The Georgian Room

*Four Seasons Olympic Hotel*
*411 University Street*
*Downtown Seattle*
*(206) 621-7889*
*$$$*

The Georgian Room is the place to really impress your significant other! Located in the Four Seasons Hotel, it is one of the most romantic and elegant restaurants in town. This is the place to really impress your significant other! The decor is "Old-World, French chateau, British royalty." A pianist plays soft music for your enjoyment. The mood is quiet elegance, and the setting is perfect for a delicious meal and sophisticated conversation. The service is as classy as the surroundings. Dress is nice to dressy, depending on your plans for the evening.

The hotel's downtown location makes it a great pre-theater spot for dinner (The 5th Avenue is right around the corner). Typically the age range of diners is from thirty upwards, with the majority being forty. Dinner is served until 10:00 P.M. during the week and weekends until 10:30 P.M. The Georgian accepts major credit cards, but no personal checks (hotel policy). Reservations are strongly suggested.

# Il Bistro

*93A Pike Street*
*Downtown Seattle*
*(206) 682-3049*
*$$*

Voted one of the" Most Romantic Places in Seattle," Il Bistro is decorated in European style. The small bistro's dark wood and white tablecloths, flickering candles, and soft jazz make it a very romantic place. Dress ranges from casual to dressy. In general, the age of the crowd ranges from the thirties to forties.

The menu offers a variety of Italian favorites as well as Northwest salmon (in season). The bar offers its own menu of appetizers and snacks, and there is a smoking section available. This late night menu is available until 1:00 A.M. daily. After dinner hour, the bar livens up a bit. The music shifts to Motown, or early '60s and '70s classics.

Dinner hours are from 5:30 P.M. until 10:00 P.M., weeknights, and from 5:30 until 11:00 P.M. on the weekends. The bar remains open until 2:00 A.M. Il Bistro accepts all major credit cards, and personal checks, with the proper identification. Reservations are suggested for dinner.

# LeoMelina Ristorante Di Mare

*96 Union Street*
*South of the Pike Place Market*
*Seattle*
*(206) 623-3783*
*www.savvydiner.com/leomelina*
*$$$*

LeoMelina is owned and run by Leo and Melina Varchetta, natives of Naples, Italy. The restaurant has already distinguished itself from the many Italian restaurants in our city, receiving a five star rating from *The News Tribune*. The decor is subtle, romantic and beautiful. The lighting is soft, with angels suspended from each chandelier.

When weather permits, you can dine outside on the patio. Nothing is more romantic than dinner under the stars, and this is a one-of-a-kind patio restaurant. They even have heat lamps for those chilly Seattle nights. You can enjoy a full-service menu on the patio, which looks toward Alki Point and Puget Sound

Inside, enjoy live Italian opera on Friday and Saturday nights. The noise level is medium and is conducive to intimate conversations. Dress is casual to dressy. Of course, with stars such as Jack Nicholson, Sylvester Stallone, Melanie Griffith and Antonio Banderas stopping by, you might want to wear your best duds!

Incredible food and an extremely friendly waitstaff make LeoMelina a very popular spot, so make reservations for weekend nights.

## Mangoes Thai Cuisine

*1841 42nd Avenue East*
*Seattle*
*(206) 324-6467*
*$$*

Thai food seems to be *en vogue* these days, so impress your date by taking him/her to Mangoes Thai Cuisine on Capitol Hill. Mangoes serves up some of the best Phad Thai in Seattle! It is a great restaurant with a pleasant staff. During the summer months, you can dine outside on the patio. The age of diners is thirty and over. The atmosphere is relaxed, and the noise level is low so you don't have to yell to be heard.

Mangoes serves dinner from 5:00 P.M. to 9:15 P.M. weeknights and from 5:00 P.M. to 9:45 P.M. on weekends. Reservations are accepted, but not mandatory.

## Maximilien in the Market

*81A Pike Street*
*Pike Place Market (look to the left, under the clock)*
*(206) 682-7270*
*$$*

Maximilien French Café (*"un restaurant-café très Français"*) looks as if you just jet-setted over to France for dinner, and no one knows romance like the French. The all-wood decor is distinctly French, with wine bottles decorating the walls. Only the view of

Elliott Bay reminds you that you're still in Seattle, Washington. The menu is, you guessed it, French! The dinner offerings change nightly, and include fresh fish, beef, lamb, veal and other continental entrées. Monday through Thursday, a four-course meal, including soup, salad, an entrée and dessert, is available. Although French food is often rich, many of the courses are on the "light" side.

Typically, the crowd tends to be early thirties and up; however, those in their twenties will also enjoy this spot. Dress can range from casual to extremely dressy, and market-goers are as common as pre-opera diners. The air of romance is everywhere, much like Paris, and Maximiliens makes an ideal "special occasion" place to dine. Dinner is served Monday through Saturday, 5:30 until 10:00 P.M., and reservations are recommended. Brunch (menu selections) is served on Sunday from 9:30 A.M. to 4:00 P.M. Maximiliens accepts all major credit cards, but no personal checks.

# Palisade

*2601 West Marina Place*
*Elliott Bay Marina*
*(206) 285-1000*
*$$-$$$*

The combination of view, architecture and food makes this a "see-and-be-seen" restaurant and a "must" on your list. Palisade's setting is spectacular. Located at the base of Magnolia, it's right on Elliott Bay, looking back at the cityscape. (Request side-by-side seating to take full advantage of the water and city view.) The interior is a mix of Polynesian and Hawaiian themes. Saltwater pools with fish, starfish ,and lava rock greet you as you enter the restaurant. Romance fills the air, as you walk over the waterfalls and ponds, to your table.

At night, the age of the patrons is less obvious than the sense that they are well-established. Remember, this is a place to "be seen," so dress accordingly. During the day it's a mixed bag of boaters, seniors and young couples. The meals are beautifully and artistically served on pottery especially designed for Palisade. Piano music plays in the background, but not loud enough to disrupt your conversation.

The bar overlooks the restaurant, and has an outdoor deck.

On nice nights, this is a great choice for starting or finishing the evening. Try a Polynesian drink, served in elegant glasses. The bar is open until 12:30 A.M., and closes at 11:30 P.M. on Sundays.

Dinner is served from 5:00 P.M. to 10:00 P.M. Sunday through Thursday and from 5:00 P.M. to 11:00 P.M. on Friday and Saturday. Palisade accepts major credit cards and personal checks.

## The Pink Door

*1919 Post Alley*
*Inside the Soames-Dunn Building*
*Pike Place Market*
*(206) 443-3241*

This Italian soul food restaurant can only be found by, you guessed it, its pink door. Located on Post Alley, the Pink Door has no sign, just that pink door as its well-known landmark. Inside, the European setting is charming. The atmosphere is romantic, with candles on the floral tablecloths and on the deck as well. The outdoor seating comes fully equipped with a view of Puget Sound. The restaurant serves a four-course Italian dinner which changes weekly. This meal, and the manner in which it is served, makes for an impressive date.

The Pink Door attracts all age groups, but the majority are twenty five and over. During the warmer months, sitting out on the deck, under the stars, makes for a wonderfully romantic night. The Pink Door also features nightly music. Reservations are a must, especially if you want to sit outside. Dinner begins at 5:30 and the last serving is at 10:00 P.M. Bar service is á la carte. The Pink Door accepts major credit cards and cash only.

## Place Pigalle

*81 Pike Street*
*In the Pike Place Market*
*(206) 624-1756*
*$$*

Located in a far corner of the Pike Place Market, this well-loved, intimate hideaway has been here since 1982. The views of Elliott Bay and the mountains are spectacular. To find it, go behind the fish market near the clock; the restaurant sits toward the water and below the main level of the market. The black-and-white checkered floor, wood chairs and white tablecloths create a sophisticated atmosphere, and the fresh flowers and candles on each table exude romance. But the view eclipses the decor. You'll enjoy watching the ships come in and out of the harbor, with Alki Point as background. Honored by the *Wine Spectator*, the restaurant is well-known for its wine and champagne list.

The menu offers French/Mediterranean dishes, including seafood, beef, lamb, chicken and salads. Diners are mostly mid-thirties and older, and tend to have a sophisticated appreciation for food and wine. Place Pigalle serves dinner from 5:30 P.M. to 10:00 P.M. Monday through Thursday, 6:00 P.M. to 11:00 P.M. Friday and Saturday, and is closed Sundays. They take all major credit cards and personal checks.

# Prego

*515 Madison Street*
*Renaissance Madison Hotel*
*Downtown Seattle*
*(206) 583-0300*
*$$*

Perched on the top of the Madison Hotel, Prego is an excellent Italian restaurant with a terrific view. The romantic atmosphere greets you from the moment you walk in. The colors are soft and heavy-on-the-mauve, and the lights are dim. Tables are draped with white tablecloths. The tone is quiet and relaxed, and encourages intimate conversation. The incredible views of the city, Elliott Bay and Lake Union make a perfect backdrop. The menu offers Italian and contemporary Northwest cuisine, and the entrées look as good as they taste. The age of the diners varies greatly due to the fact that the restaurant is located in a hotel, but the typical age is twenty-five and older. Some couples dress up for a meal at Prego's, but office attire is also perfect.

Dinner is served from 5:30 P.M. to 10:00 P.M. during the week, and until 11:00 P.M. on the weekends. Prego accepts all major credit cards and personal checks, with the proper identification. Reservations are strongly suggested, especially when the weather is nice.

# The Queen Mary

*2912 NE 55th Street*
*Just off NE 25th, near University Village*
*(206) 527-2770*
*$-$$*

Walking into the Queen Mary is like stepping into a room in an English castle. The floral curtains and elegant chairs create a cozy, yet aristocratic atmosphere. Never mind the royal ambiance, "anything goes" perfectly describes the dress of the customers. People in jeans drop by for an espresso, while a tux and formal-clad couple stop in for dinner before the ballet. Afternoon tea is served daily, from 2:00 to 5:00 P.M., and includes tortes, tarts, scones, crumpets, fruits, sorbets, sandwiches, teacakes, and more. This is a great place for an afternoon interlude, as many couples have discovered, and you won't have to plan dinner. Conversations over tea is a great way to get to know someone.

After-dinner visits are also popular, and the desserts are as delicious as their aroma promises. All kinds of espresso and teas are available, day and night. Queen Mary is a wonderful place to just talk; the music is quiet, and the fare is excellent. Dinner is served Tuesday, Wednesday and Thursday from 5:00 to 9:00 P.M., and Friday and Saturday from 5:00 to 10:00 P.M.

# Ray's Boathouse

*6049 Seaview Avenue NW*
*Seattle*
*(206) 789-3770*
*$$$-$$$$*

Ray's Boathouse sits right on the water and has a spectacular view of Shilshole Bay—breathtaking and romantic! The menu offers delicious seafood, fresh from the Pacific Northwest. Plan your dinner around sunset, so you can truly enjoy the romance of a Seattle sunset. The sun setting over the Sound is one of nature's perfect gifts, and you can enjoy it with someone special. The service is excellent and the atmosphere is relaxed and casual. The bar upstairs is a lot of fun and serves great appetizers.

# Reiner's

*1106 Eighth Avenue*
*Seattle*
*(206) 624-2222*
*$$$-$$$$*

Reiner's has the perfect combination of Old World service, European charm, and classic continental cuisine. The restaurant is small, elegant and intimate. Sit underneath the vaulted ceiling and hanging chandelier and dine on some of the best food in the city. The personal service is attentive and courteous, and you'll feel like royalty. The menu consists of scrumptious meals, for example, Chicken Breast topped with Dungeness Crab or linguini with Italian hard smoked salmon. Reiner's also offers an impressive and extensive wine list, with a large selection of champagne and sparkling wine. The separate dessert menu is to die for. Although the menu includes appetizing selections such as bread pudding and chocolate mousse, I suggest the Sampler Dessert Plate, so you can try a bit of everything! Attire is dressy and the crowd is thirty and older.

Dinner is served from 5:30 P.M. to 9:00 P.M. Tuesday through Saturday and reservations are strongly suggested. Reiner's was rated the Number One restaurant by *The Seattle Times*, so check it out with someone special!

# Rover's

*2808 E Madison*
*Seattle*
*(206) 325-7442*
*$$$-$$$$*

Rover's is a romantic spot tucked away in a beautiful, peaceful courtyard. If you enter from Madison Avenue, you can stroll hand-in-hand through a peaceful patio. If you enter from 28th, the white picket fence gives you the feeling of going to Mom's house for dinner. The relaxed atmosphere, combined with the dramatic lighting and pastel art, makes for a unique dining experience. When weather permits, enjoy eating on the outdoor patio. Rover's serves up delicious continental cuisine including selections of fish, rabbit and lobster. The noise level is quiet to moderate, so you can enjoy good conversation along with good food.

## The Salish Lodge

*Snoqualmie Falls*
*Snoqualmie (40 minutes east of Seattle, off I-90)*
*Toll-free, (800) 826-6124, or (206) 888-2556*
*Breakfast and Lunch: $-$$*
*Dinner: $$-$$$*

New York's Niagara Falls may be too far away for a romantic dinner, but Snoqualmie Falls is just around the corner. North Bend is a scenic drive from Seattle. The Salish Lodge is located right at the crest of the 268-foot falls, which are actually 100 feet higher than Niagara. You can walk down to the falls, but be sure to wear comfortable shoes. The restaurant serves a five-course country breakfast, and lunch and dinner. The age range of diners changes with the meals. Breakfast attracts all ages, while the evening clientele tend to be in the thirties and forties.

Breakfast is a big draw, and is served from 7:00 A.M. to 11:00 A.M. Monday through Friday and from 7:00 A.M. to 2:45 P.M. Saturday and Sunday. Specials such as Country Breakfast and Morning Elegance will fill your stomach, while the friendly atmosphere will fill your heart.

Lunch is served from 11:30 A.M. to 2:45 P.M. Monday through Sunday. Saturday and Sunday, it is served upstairs in the Attic Lounge (age twenty-one and over only). Lunch is a nice option, because you still have the light to see the view of the gorge and the river, and it's much less expensive than the evening meal. The dress is casual during the day.

Dinner is a more romantic atmosphere, and most couples plan an outside walk to view the falls, which are lit. Although there is no dress code, diners tend to dress up more in the evening. The fare is Northwest cuisine, and features salmon, quail, rabbit, and veal. Dinner is served from 5:00 P.M. to 9:45 P.M. every night.

Couples over twenty-one should consider a walk, with an appetizer break in the Attic Lounge. This is without question one of the most stunning views in the area, and the comfortable couches and overall cozy country atmosphere makes for a delightful respite from the rush of city life. Besides a large selection of appetizers, the Lounge can also order up any of the 740 bottled wines and champagnes from the Salish Wine Cellar, 200 of which are from Northwest vintners.

Reservations are required, and you will want to make them at least four weeks in advance—sometimes up to three months, depending on the season, the meal and the day. The Salish Lodge does not take personal checks, but does accept major credit cards.

# Salty's on Alki

*1936 Harbor SW*
*West Seattle Waterfront*
*(206) 937-1600*
*$$-$$$ (Market Price)*

Salty's is literally *over* the water. Jutting out on the east side of Alki Point, it has one of the most romantic views in the city. You can sit and watch the sunset as it reflects off the Seattle city skyline, then watch as the lights come on with the rising moon. The interior capitalizes on this breathtaking view. The decor is simple, yet elegant, with candles on the white linen-dressed tables. Attire is nice to dressy, and at night mostly dressy. The typical age of diners ranges from thirty to fifty-plus, although high school proms always bring in teens. The specialties are seafood and pasta, with steak and chicken on the menu as well.

After dinner, take your date on a romantic moonlit stroll along the boardwalk. The walk is paved, and high-heel-friendly if you don't overdo it.

Dinner is served from 5:00 P.M. to 10:00 P.M. Monday through Thursday, from 5:00 P.M. to 10:30 P.M. on Friday, from 4:30 P.M. to 10:30 P.M. on Saturday, and from 4:30 P.M. to 10:00 P.M. on Sunday. Reservations are required, but especially if you want a seat right at the window and at sunset. Salty's accepts all major credit cards and personal checks with the proper ID.

# Serafina

*2043 Eastlake Avenue E*
*Seattle*
*(206) 323-0807*
*$$-$$$*

This rustic Euro-Italian restaurant and bar combines romance and fun. When weather permits, you can eat outside in the cozy, secluded patio. Inside, the restaurant is comfortable, with white linen and soft candlelight on the tables. You can enjoy live music Wednesday through Saturday, but even with the music, the noise level is quiet enough to talk. The bar can get lively, mostly filled with neighborhood locals, and the dress is "typical Seattle trendy/casual." The food here is really good, the service and dining cozy. Serafina is proud of their wine selection and impressive espresso menu.

Dinner is served from 5:30 P.M. until 10:00 P.M. weeknights, and is open until 11:00 P.M. on Friday and Saturday nights. Make reservations, because there can be a wait on the weekends.

# Sorrento Hotel

*900 Madison*
*Capitol Hill/Downtown*
*Hotel:(206) 622-6400 or (800) 426-1265 (hotel)*
*(206) 343-6156 (Hunt Club restaurant)*
*$$-$$$*

Treat your special someone to the most romantic evening of his/her life at the Sorrento Hotel. From the moment you arrive, you'll experience Old-World romance and elegance. On warm evenings, cocktails and appetizers are served outside on the terrace. You can sit beneath umbrella-covered tables beside the beautiful Italian fountain, while sipping a cool drink.

If a superb dinner is in the plan, move inside to the Hunt Club restaurant. Brick walls, Honduran mahogany woodwork, and soft music combine with white linen, fresh flowers and candle-lit tables to create an atmosphere designed for gazing into your tablemate's eyes. Champagne buckets sit nearby for toasting any celebration. You'll find the waitstaff warm and attentive, never stuffy or rushed. Dress tends towards the dressy side. The age of patrons generally ranges from the late twenties to seniors. If the evening would not be complete without flowers, call ahead and "Whims," the Sorrento's in-house florist, will make sure you have fresh flowers (a bouquet, a corsage or a single rose) on your table. Valet parking is complimentary with brunch, lunch or dinner.

Dinner is served from 5:30 P.M. to 10:00 P.M. Sunday through Thursday, and from 5:30 P.M. to 11:00 P.M. Friday and Saturday. The Sorrento accepts major credit cards and personal checks with proper ID. Reservations are a must!

After a wonderful meal, why not sit and talk in the Fireside Room? Decorated with velvet love-seats and a huge fireplace, this lounge is like no other in the city. During the cooler months, this is a particularly fine place to sip an after dinner drink, or espresso. The Fireside Lounge is open until 2:00 A.M. Monday through Saturday, and until midnight on Sundays. There is a pianist to add to the mood Wednesday through Saturday.

## Sostanza Trattoria

*1927 43rd Avenue E*
*Madison Park/Seattle*
*(206) 324-9701*
*$$$*

Sostanza sits at the end of East Madison Avenue and has a view of Lake Washington. This small, cozy restaurant serves Northern Central Italian cuisine and delicious homemade desserts. Entrées include salads, pasta dishes, risotto seafood, and quail. The patio is open during the warm summer months, and the view of Lake Washington is breathtaking. After, or before dinner, take a stroll along East Madison and do a little window-shopping, or stop for espresso. (See chapter 4, *Noteworthy Neighborhoods*, for more information on Madison Park). You can also walk over to the park and beach to look at the lake under the stars.

Sostanza is very popular, so make reservations by Wednesday for weekend nights.

# The Space Needle Restaurants
# The Emerald Suite

*Seattle Center*
*(206) 443-2100 or (800) 937-9582*
*$$-$$$*

If you want to make that special someone feel on top of the world, plan dinner in the Emerald Suite at the 500-foot level of the Space Needle. This elegant (and relatively formal at night) restaurant rotates 360 degrees, allowing you to watch the city view turn into lake view, mountain view and Puget Sound view, and then start all over again. It was also voted "Seattle's Favorite Special Occasion Restaurant." The ages of the clientele range from twenties to seniors, and there is a dress code; no jeans, tee shirts or tennis shoes allowed. Reservations are required. Dinner is served Monday through Saturday from 4:00 P.M. to 10:45 P.M., and Sunday from 5:00 P.M. to 10:45 P.M.

For a less formal option—*i.e.*, no dress code—try the Space Needle Restaurant at the 500-foot level. Entrées in this adjacent dining room cost less, but the same excellent seafood, beef and chicken specialties are on the menu. After your meal, stroll around the observation deck and buy a souvenir for your beloved.

The Space Needle accepts major credit cards and in-state checks with identification.

# Yarrow Bay Grille

*1270 Carillon Point*
*Kirkland*
*(425) 889-9052*
*$$-$$$*

The Yarrow Bay Grille is a very romantic restaurant. In fact, a marriage proposal or two is not uncommon during the dinner hour. The restaurant is located above the Yarrow Bay Marina, and every table has a water view. You can watch boat activity while you dine.

At night, there are candles on the tables and long, white tablecloths. The menu changes daily and includes seafood and steak entrées.

Diners range from age twenty-five and up, and the atmosphere is quiet and relaxed. Most people are dressed up, but casual dress is acceptable as well. After dinner, take a stroll around the grounds of the Woodmark Hotel, or take the paved path along Lake Washington. Dinner is served from 5:30 to 10:00 P.M. Monday through Saturday, and 5:00 to 9:00 P.M. Sunday. Reservations are suggested, especially if you want to catch the sunset. The Yarrow Bay Grille accepts credit cards and personal checks.

## SOPHISTICATED RESTAURANTS

## Benihana

*1200 Fifth Avenue*
*IBM Building/Seattle*
*(206) 682-4686*
*$$$*

Benihana is a unique and sophisticated dining experience. The food is cooked at your table; in fact, your table actually surrounds a hot grille on which your dinner is prepared. With deft skill, your personal chef chops, prepares and cooks your choice of entrées while you watch. Selections include: seafood, a vegetarian meal, Teriyaki steak and chicken, Hibachi chicken, scallops, prawns, lobster, and numerous combinations. Benihana is a lot of fun and the food and service is extraordinary. You won't find a lot of privacy here; you may even share your table with strangers, but that adds to the fun of the evening. The restaurant is down the street from The 5th Avenue Theatre, so it's perfect for a pre-theater date. Dress ranges from casual to "Theater Dressy," and people of all ages dine here. There is entertainment in the lounge on Friday or Saturday nights.

Benihana serves dinner from 5:30 P.M. to 10:00 P.M. Monday through Thursday, 5:30 P.M. to 11:00 P.M. Friday, 5:00 P.M. to 11:00 P.M. Saturday, and 4:30 P.M. to 9:30 P.M. Sunday. Reservations are strongly recommended, because Benihana is a very popular restaurant!

# Canlis

*2576 Aurora Avenue N*
*Seattle*
*(206) 283-3313*
*www.canlis.com*
*$$$$-$$$$$ (Market Price)*

Canlis was opened in 1950 by Peter Canlis and soon became "the grandest restaurant in Seattle since the roaring '20s." With a stunning view of Lake Union, it still is a grand restaurant. The atmosphere is upscale, classy and sophisticated. The food is regional Mediterranean, and the entrées are good-sized. Selections of steak, seafood and chicken all are offered. Dim lighting and fresh flowers on each table create a romantic atmosphere. Live piano music plays nightly, but not so loud as to disrupt a private conversation. If this isn't enough, the service is warm and friendly. The Canlis crowd is primarily forty and older; however, a younger couple will not feel out of place. You'll definitely want to dust off your best outfit for this evening together.

Canlis starts dinner at 5:00 P.M. Closing time varies. Usually, the last reservation is 9:30 P.M. on Friday and Saturday nights, but it can be later. Reservations are required, so call in advance.

# Dahlia Lounge

*1904 Fourth Avenue*
*Seattle*
*(206) 682-4142*
*$$$*

If you and your date know and enjoy good food and fine restaurants, you must try the Dahlia Lounge, where the food is artistically presented  in a comfortable setting. The neon "Cafe" sign gives you the feeling of New York City at night. The restaurant is dark, with candles lighting each table and the glow reflecting off the mirrored walls. The high ceiling and mirrored walls make the restaurant appear larger than it really is. The upstairs balcony tables are fun for "people watching." The noise level is moderate, so you can still enjoy each other's company. The crowd here is sophisticated and ranges from thirty up. Dress is casual to nice (mind you, I didn't see any cut-off jeans), but you'll see jeans and suits sitting next to each other.

The Dahlia Lounge serves dinner from 5:30 P.M. to 10:00 P.M. Monday through Thursday, from 5:15 P.M. to 11:00 P.M. Friday and Saturday, and from 5:00 P.M. to 10:00 P.M. Sunday. Reservations are recommended.

## Daniel's Broiler

*10500 NE 8th*
*Bellevue Place*
*(425) 462-4662*
*$$*

Located in the same complex that houses the Hyatt Hotel, Daniel's Broiler is one of the few "view" restaurants in Bellevue. The high wooden booths and candle-lit tables make for a romantic setting. The view of Bellevue and Lake Washington is spectacular, and on a clear night you can see Seattle. The atmosphere is quiet and relaxed. The food is very good.

The adjoining bar is mellow, and every Sunday night features a popular Jazz Showcase. If you love jazz, you can enjoy live music every Sunday from 7:00 P.M. to 11:00 P.M. The Sunday Jazz Showcase can get very busy, so plan to arrive early.

The casual, yet upscale atmosphere of Daniel's Broiler draws a thirty to fifty-ish crowd. This is definitely a place to impress a date. Dress is eclectic; some people dress up, others are very casual.

Dinner is served from 5:30 to 10:00 P.M. Monday through Thursday; from 5:30 to 11:00 P.M. Friday and Saturday; and from 5:00 to 10:00 P.M. on Sunday. Major credit cards and personal checks accepted.

There is another Daniel's Broiler located at 200 Lake Washington Boulevard, Seattle, (206) 329-4191. It offers the same great food and decor as the Bellevue location, but does not have music.

# El Gaucho

*2505 First Avenue*
*Belltown/Seattle*
*(206) 728-1337*

Walking into El Gaucho for the first time is an experience in itself! The restaurant is located in an inconspicuous green building in the Belltown district. Once inside, you'll feel as if you stepped into the roaring '20s. The tables are on levels, with white tablecloths, candles and fresh flowers. The owner describes El Gaucho as a "place to spend the evening." Live music plays seven nights a week, and the charcoal-burning grill serves up some of the best meat dishes in the city! If you enjoy a good cigar or would like to join the growing trend, try El Gaucho's cigar room, hailed as "Seattle's Finest Cigar Room." Dress is typically "dressy-casual" but this is a place to be seen, so dress to impress!

El Gaucho serves dinner from 5:00 P.M. to 1:00 A.M. every night. It is a great late night dinner date restaurant. Though there are plenty of tables, they fill up quickly. Reservations are a must.

# Ernie's Bar and Grille

*2411 Alaskan Way/Edgewater Hotel*
*Waterfront*
*Seattle*
*(206) 728-7000*
*$$ (market prices)*

Ernie's Bar and Grille is located in The Edgewater, Seattle's only waterfront hotel. This unique lounge is built on pilings, so you actually sit over the water. With its floor-to-ceiling picture windows, enjoying a meal here makes you feel as if you're dining aboard a cruise ship. The restaurant is decorated in soft greens and light wood. A brick fireplace helps create a mellow atmosphere. Ernie's serves Northwest cuisine and specializes in fresh seafood. Sunday brunch here is a great way to start a day date. Typically, diners are twenty-five and older; however prom dates are a common sight in the spring. Dress tends to be on the dressy side. Parking is validated by the hotel if you park in their lot. Reservations are a must.

The bar is more casual, and very low-key, and has the same

large windows and sweeping view of Puget Sound and Alki Point. You can sit and enjoy a drink, while watching the ferry boats glide through Elliott Bay. The bar features piano, but the music is not overbearing. Tuesday nights, "blues in the bar" plays from 8:30 P.M. to 12:30 A.M.

Dinner is served in the restaurant from 5:00 P.M. to 9:30 P.M. every night. Ernie's Bar and Grille accepts all major credit cards and personal checks.

## Flying Fish

*2234 First Avenue*
*Belltown/Seattle*
*(206) 728-8595*
*www.flyingfishseattle.com*
*$$*

The Flying Fish is a great bar and restaurant for a casual, yet impressive meal. The decor is modern, with big windows that open onto the street. Dine on the patio or in a booth, and enjoy the small view of Puget Sound. The restaurant has an "art-deco" feeling and an open kitchen. The upstairs balcony provides a great perch for people-watching, while the booths are cozier. The clientele is twenty-one and older and the dress is casual, but cool. The noise level is moderate, but might be louder in the lively bar area. There is an excellent selection of fresh seafood dishes. The desserts are mouth-watering, with treats such as Chocolate Chip Angel Food Cake with fudge rum sauce and espresso ice cream. Dessert is served until 1:00 A.M., so go ahead and indulge that late-night sweet tooth. This is a late-night date spot that must be visited!

The Flying Fish serves dinner from 5:00 P.M. to 12:00 midnight, every night of the week. For late diners they offer a delicious late night menu. Both it and the dessert menu are served until 1:00 A.M. The bar closes at 2:00 A.M. Reservations are recommended.

# Kamon on Lake Union

*1177 Fairview Avenue N*
*West Lake Union*
*(206) 622-4665*
*$$*

Kamon on Lake Union is really three restaurants in one. There is a sushi bar, the Pacific Rim dining room, and a Teppan dining room. The sushi bar is ideal for a casual date. If you enjoy this delicacy, you can sit right at the bar to observe the preparation, or do without watching and sit at tables. If sushi isn't your thing, try the Pacific Rim, which serves international cuisine. Northwest favorites are included on the menu. In the Teppan dining room, your food is cooked right in front of you, like Benihana of Tokyo (which is owned by the same company).

Obviously, Kamon has something to fit any occasion. There is a Piano Bar with live music every Thursday through Saturday, from 7:30 to 11:30 P.M. The restaurant is elegant Oriental design and the dress tends to run from casual to dressy. The sushi bar is much more casual then the other two dining rooms. The typical age range of diners is from mid-twenties to late thirties—the very crowd that we have to thank for the popularization of sushi! There is a beautiful view of Lake Union, and you can eat outside on the deck during the summer.

Dinner is served from 5:00 P.M. to 10:00 P.M. Sunday through Thursday, and from 5:00 P.M. to 11:00 P.M. Friday and Saturday. Kamon does take reservations and accepts Visa, Mastercard and American Express.

# Metropolitan Grill

*820 Second Avenue*
*Downtown Seattle*
*(206) 624-3287*
*$$*

The Metropolitan Grill claims to serve the best steak in town, and Seattleites seem to agree. The restaurant is designed to resemble a restaurant in Manhattan, or any other similarly urban and urbane setting. The booths are steeped in deep green velvet and brass. The noise level is medium-to-loud; this is a place where people talk a lot over their meals. Diners are mostly early thirties and up, owing to the fact that it's the perfect location for the city's "after-work" crowd. There is a bar which closes with the restaurant. This is most definitely an after-work watering hole. The dress is "professional." It is not uncommon for people to be dressed up and en route to the theater. There is on-street parking, or in the parking garage across the street.

The menu includes seafood, pasta, chicken and steak—"Seattle's Award Winning" variety—and excellent prime rib. The Chateaubriand for Two deserves a special note, and is carved right at your table. Dinner is served from 5:00 to 11:00 P.M. Monday through Saturday, and until 10:00 P.M. on Sundays (also open for brunch when the Seahawks play). Reservations are strongly suggested. The Metropolitan Grill accepts all major credit cards, and personal checks with proper identification.

## Morgan's Lake Place Bistro

*2 Lake Bellevue Drive*
*Off Bel-Red Road at 120th Street*
*(425) 455-2244*

Morgan's Lake Place Bistro sits on beautiful Lake Bellevue, Bellevue's only urban lake (sometimes called "fake lake," although the water and the ducks are quite real). Outdoor seating is available during the warmer months, and you are right on the water. During the day, you can watch the ducks and geese paddling about on the lake. Inside, the atmosphere is casual and almost rustic. You and your companion will enjoy a relaxed and comfortable dinner.

Morgan's is one of the most successful Eastside restaurants; their formula is high-quality, well-priced food (pastas, seafood, poultry, beef, salads, appetizers) and great service in a pleasant environment. The music is soft and the lights are dim. The typical age of diners ranges from about thirty to fifty-plus, although everyone in between is seen and welcome (including kids). Dress is casual to nice.

Dinner is served from 5:30 to 9:00 P.M. Sunday through Saturday and until 10:00 P.M. on Friday nights, and the bar is open until 1:00 A.M. The lounge has its followers, mostly from the professional crowd. Reservations are suggested and Morgan's accepts major credit cards.

# Nikko

*1900 Fifth Avenue*
*The Westin Hotel*
*Seattle*
*(206) 322-4641*
*http:/seattle.uspan.com/nikko/*
*$$$*

    Nikko serves traditional Japanese food in authentic surroundings. The restaurant includes a sushi bar where you can sit and watch the chef cook. The tables are well-spaced, and the noise level moderate, so you can still talk quietly. The lighting is medium to dark. Dress is casual to dressy, and people of all ages dine here. The menu includes Teriyaki specialties, seafood, sushi and egg-rolls. Centrally located in The Westin Hotel, Nikko is in a prime position for the theater or anything else in downtown Seattle. Nikko also makes a great lunch date, serving all-you-can-eat Sushi from 11:30 A.M. to 2:00 P.M. weekdays.

    Nikko serves dinner from 5:30 P.M. until 10:00 P.M. and Happy Hour in the bar runs from 5:00 P.M. until 7:00 P.M. Reservations for dinner are advised.

# ObaChine

*1518 Sixth Avenue*
*Downtown Seattle*
*(206) 749-9653*
*$$*

    Wolfgang Puck and wife, Barbara Lazaroff, are the owners of this Pan-Asian restaurant. The entrées are dramatic and colorful, as well as delicious! The restaurant is very dramatic with deep purple carpets, artwork on the walls and tables, and an open-tile kitchen upstairs. ObaChine also has a Sushi Bar downstairs. The restaurant is impressive, dramatic and has a New York feel about it. You'll find people of all ages here, but most are twenty-something and older. Dress is casual, but trendy and cool. All of this style comes reasonably priced, and the location is ideal for dining before the theater, after shopping downtown, or for a plain old great night on the town in the heart of the city.

ObaChine serves dinner from 5:30 P.M. until 10:00 P.M. every night. Dinner reservations are strongly suggested.

## Palomino Bistro

*1420 Fifth Avenue*
*(Fifth and Pike)*
*Downtown Seattle*
*(206) 623-1300*
*$$$*

Palomino is located in one of Seattle's most beautiful buildings, the US Bank Center and City Centre Building. The restaurant is on the third floor, overlooking the atrium. The decor is casual, but classy, and the food is excellent. The Mediterranean/Northwest menu includes spit-roasted dishes, pasta, grilled food cooked in the Applewood Grill, Roma Style Pizzas and more. The entire dining room is smoke-free, but smoking is permitted in the lounge. Dress is casual to business, but the after-work crowd can be dressier. The noise level is moderate to noisy, due to the open atrium. Ask for a table in the back if you're looking for a quiet spot to dine, or a table near the atrium wall to enjoy the city lights.

Palomino serves dinner from 5:30 P.M. to 9:30 P.M. Monday through Thursday, from 5:30 P.M. to 10:30 P.M. Friday and Saturday, and from 5:00 P.M. to 9:30 P.M. Sunday. Reservations should be made for dinner, especially if you are requesting a particular table.

## The Poor Italian Cafe

*2000 Second Avenue (at Virginia)*
*Downtown Seattle*
*(206) 441-4313*
*$-$$*

The Poor Italian Cafe's motto is, "You'll feel rich with the taste of Italy." But you don't have to be rich to enjoy this restaurant. This is an ideal date spot because of the pleasant ambiance and reasonable prices. With its tile floors, brick walls and white linen tablecloths, the café looks as if it might sit on a street in Italy. At night, when the lights go down and Italian music plays softly in the background, the restaurant can be very romantic. You'll feel as if you and your date have flown to Italy for the night. Dress ranges from casual to very dressy, and everything in between.

Its downtown location makes the Poor Italian a nice "pre-theater" spot. The crowd tends to be a combination of the after-work group and a little younger. Diners range in age from twenty-one to thirty-five. There is a small, adjoining bar, which is fairly quiet and mostly used by customers while waiting for a table. Smoking is available in designated areas only.

Dinner is served from 4:00 P.M. to 10:00 P.M. Monday through Thursday; from 4:00 P.M. to 11:00 P.M. Friday and Saturday; and from 4:30 P.M. to 9:00 P.M. on Sunday. Reservations are suggested, if you don't want to wait for a table. All major credit cards and personal checks are accepted with the proper identification.

## Raga Cuisine of India

*555 108th NE*
*Downtown Bellevue*
*(425) 450-0336*
*$$*

The purpose of Raga is to take care of you and to share with you the culture of India. The restaurant serves all types of Indian food. You'll find lamb, chicken, vegetable dishes and seafood. The atmosphere is nice, with white tablecloths and hanging plants. This small and intimate place, located in a tiny building tucked away among the skyscrapers of downtown Bellevue. Drive slowly on 108th, or you'll speed right past it! Dress is fairly dressy and the crowd is thirty and older. However, even if you're twenty, the friendly waitstaff will make you feel right at home. For a luncheon date, try Raga's lunch buffet, served Friday through Sunday.

Raga Cuisine of India serves dinner from 5:00 P.M. to 10:00 P.M. every night. Reservations are a good idea for weekend nights.

# Ristorante Il Bacio

*16564 Cleveland Street*
*Redmond*
*(253) 839-7277*
*$$-$$$*

Ristorante Il Bacio is a great find, tucked away in a small brick-walled mall. Master Chef Rino Baglio, a native of Como, Italy, is world-renowned, and has served the likes of Princess Caroline of Monaco, Prince Charles, Princess Diana, and former president Ronald Reagan. The food here is authentic Italian, with a wonderful selection of pasta, chicken, veal and seafood. The service is excellent and the atmosphere comfortable. Il Bacio was awarded four-and-one-half stars by the *Journal American,* and five stars in the Who's Who national directory. Dress is casual to dressy and diners are from the mid-twenties and up. This is not far from the Microsoft campus, so expect to see the Microsoft crowd there during lunch. Come to Il Bacio for delicious Italian food and a wonderful night together.

Il Bacio serves dinner from 5:00 P.M. to 9:00 P.M. Monday through Saturday. Lunch is served Monday through Friday from 11:30 A.M. to 2:00 P.M. Reservations are highly recommended.

# Roy's

*1900 Fifth Avenue*
*The Westin Hotel*
*(206) 256-7697*
*www.hawaii~dining.com/roys/*
*$$$*

Roy's is part of Roy Yamaguchi Enterprises, a national chain owned by chef Roy Yamaguchi, a native of Tokyo. The food is Euro-Asian, with Japanese and Hawaiian influences. Every night you can choose an item featured on the "chef's nightly special" sheet. There is always something new, creative and exciting to try. All dishes are beautiful, and artistically presented. You can order chicken, fish, meat, dim-sum and some really exciting pizzas. Roy's "Melting Hot" Chocolate Soufflé needs advance notice to prepare, but is worth the calorie count! Roy's is located in the beautiful

Westin Hotel. The atmosphere is relaxed and has a Hawaiian feeling to it. Dress ranges from casual to dressy, but anything goes. The bar upstairs serves a full dinner menu, but you need to be over twenty-one to dine.

Roy's serves dinner nightly from 5:30 P.M. until 9:30 P.M. (The last reservation is taken at 9:00 P.M. and the restaurant closes at 10:00 P.M.). Reservations are recommended.

## Salute of Bellevue

*10134 Main Street*
*Old Main/Bellevue*
*(425) 688-7613*
*$$-$$$*

The outside of Salute of Bellevue looks like a restaurant in an Italian village, with archways and stonework. Inside, you'll discover beautiful arches, wood floors, white linen, candlelight, and Italian collectibles. The delicious menu and outstanding wine list makes Salute a great Eastside dating spot. The entrées are good-sized, so bring your appetite. Salute also has a delectable dessert menu, so don't fill up on dinner! You can enjoy live opera Saturday nights from 8:00 P.M. to 9:30 P.M. The crowd here is over twenty-one, and dress is casual to dressy. During the summer months, enjoy outside seating, along the sidewalk. After dinner, enjoy a stroll along Main Street, browsing the shops.

Dinner is served from 5:00 P.M. to 9:00 P.M. Monday through Thursday and 5:00 P.M. to 11:00 P.M. Friday and Saturday. Reservations are strongly recommended because Salute has become one of Bellevue's hot spots!

## Spazzo Mediterranean Grill

*10655 NE 4th*
*Key Bank Building*
*Downtown Bellevue*
*(425) 454-8255*

Spazzo Mediterranean Grill is nine flights up, with a breathtaking and romantic view. The ambiance is fun and lively. The colorful, brightly painted walls and open-style kitchen makes this a great first-date spot. At night, you can enjoy the lights of the city, or come early for a spectacular sunset. The menu offers dishes using the spit-roasting method of rotisserie cooking. A favorite is tapas, a small dish originating from Spanish taverns. Tapas Bar is noisy and fun, with the same great view. Spazzo makes a great pre-movie spot or for drinks after a Bellevue show.

Spazzo serves dinner from 4:00 P.M. to 10:00 P.M. Sunday through Thursday and from 4:00 P.M. to 11:00 P.M. Friday and Saturday. Reservations are recommended.

## Wild Ginger Asian Restaurant

*1400 Western Avenue*
*Seattle*
*(206) 623-4450*
*$$$*

Wild Ginger Asian Restaurant and Satay Bar is one of Seattle's great hot spots! The Asian cuisine includes Vietnamese, Thai and Korean dishes. The restaurant has a warm atmosphere and a humming satay bar. The food is delicious and very different from the typical Seattle cuisine. Wild Ginger is right near the Pike Place Market, so you can wander through the market and end up here for dinner. The Satay Bar is worth a trip itself. Always crowded and always fun, Wild Ginger has a loyal following. The lighting is dark so you can have a romantic meal, if you wish. The service is prompt, friendly and relaxed.

Wild Ginger serves dinner from 5:00 P.M. until 11:00 P.M. on weeknights and from 5:00 P.M. until 12:00 midnight on Friday and Saturday. Wild Ginger accepts cash and credit cards, but doesn't accept checks. Make reservations because the restaurant has loyal customers and long waits!

# Chapter Three

# Tours &
# Attractions

lthough many of us are Seattle locals, not all of us have taken advantage of the many things this fine city has to offer. For those new to the area, Seattle is a city with surprises around every corner. One of the great things about living here is that you'll never run out of new things to do, either on a date or with a friend. All you need is an open mind, a little adventure in your heart, and someone to go exploring with you. So call that someone special, tell them to put on their favorite jeans and tennis shoes, you are going exploring. . . .

# Authentic Carriages of Washington

*Downtown Seattle*
*(206) 545-2849 or (206) 825-6142*
*(206) 807-4624 (pager)*

A romantic horse-drawn carriage is an exciting and original means of transportation, and a great way to see the city. After all, anyone can take a taxi to dinner, but only someone with class and a creative imagination takes a carriage ride through the busy streets. Authentic Carriages of Washington specializes in weddings, special events, and citywide tours, so call the office and plan the date of a lifetime!

# Ferry Boat Rides

*Washington State Ferry System*
*(800) 843-3779 or (206) 464-6400 (information/schedules)*

A trip on a Washington State Ferry can provide many pleasures. Bring a picnic and enjoy the waterfront parks. Take bicycles, and explore the "island countryside." Boats leave from Seattle, Edmonds, Mukilteo and Fauntleroy. A nice trip is from Seattle to Bainbridge Island. The little one-plus street town formerly called Winslow is easy to explore and has some interesting stops and shops. For dinner, the Saltwater Cafe (403 Madison) is right down on the waterfront marina. A popular breakfast spot is the Streamliner (397 Winslow East), which is on the main drag. Poulsbo is a quaint destination village about 12 miles away. It's a nice bike ride. Vashon Island (take the Fauntleroy ferry) also offers scenic bike touring, island shopping and good food options. Check the newspaper for sunset times and enjoy a breathtaking and romantic view of the Seattle skyline and Cascade Mountains in hues of pink and orange. If the weather is chilly, warm up with a Starbucks espresso, served right on the ferry boats! Hey, it wouldn't be Seattle without the java!

# Hot Air Balloon Flights

A romantic and fun date outing is a hot air balloon ride over the scenic Sammamish Valley (home of Chateau Ste. Michelle, Columbia Winery, and Redhook Brewery). For a great combination, try a winery tour and a balloon ride. From high above the stress of the world, you and your date or friend will enjoy panoramic views of the Seattle skyline, Mt. Rainier, and the other beauties of the Puget Sound. Many balloon companies offer sunset flights, picnics, and champagne. Spend quality time together, floating above the trees and enjoying each other's company. Here are two great hot air balloon companies:

**Balloon Depot**

*16238 NE 87th*
*Redmond*
*(425) 881-9699*

**Over the Rainbow**

*14481 Woodinville-Redmond Road*
*Woodinville*
*(425) 364-0995*

# Omnidome

*Pier 59/Next to the Seattle Aquarium*
*Waterfront*
*Seattle*
*(206) 622-1868 ( information line)*
*$*

If you think bigger is better, the Omnidome is the place to go! Recent shows include *The Eruption of Mount St. Helen's: Then and Now*; *The Magic Egg: A Computer Odyssey*; *The Great Barrier Reef*; *Speed: The Ultimate Big Screen Experience*; and *The Living Sea*. The giant 70mm film is projected onto a 180-degree curved dome screen, so that you feel as if you're part of the movie. Six speakers surround you with 1,200 watts of sound. You sit, well actually lie, side by side, in the center of all this excitement. Dress is very casual because you are on the floor. The crowd ranges from six to sixty-plus, and every age seems to enjoy the shows.

The movies change, so call first to find out if the topic interests you. Call the Omnidome Information Line for current showtimes. Shows run seven days a week, from 10:00 A.M. to 10:00 P.M. You can also buy a combination Aquarium and Omnidome ticket for one price, and make a day of it.

## The Seattle Aquarium

*1483 Alaskan Way/Pier 59*
*Waterfront*
*(206) 386-4320 (information line)*
*$*

Anyone who loves the sea and marine life will find the Seattle Aquarium fascinating. Wandering through the dark exhibits can even be romantic, and its location on Elliott Bay also makes the aquarium perfect for catching a sunset over the ferries and islands of Puget Sound. A rainy afternoon can be transformed into an underwater adventure, and on sunny days you can add a stroll along the busy waterfront area.

Aside from the "edutainment" of the exhibits and the marine life, the Seattle Aquarium is noted for sponsoring outdoor trips, special events, lectures and classes. Included among the many options are kayak and canoe trips, cruises and field trips, snorkeling adventures, and whale-watching. There are also special opportunities for people with kids. The Seattle Aquarium is proud to be the home of the first sea otter conceived, born and raised in captivity, and the otter exhibit is an outstanding feature.

You can become a member of the Aquarium Society, which entitles you to discounts on events sponsored by the Aquarium. (The public is invited to these events as well, at regular prices.) The Seattle Aquarium hours are: 10:00 A.M. to 7:00 P.M., Memorial Day to Labor Day, and 10:00 A.M. to 5:00 P.M., Labor Day to Memorial Day.

## Spirit of Washington Dinner Train

*625 South 4th Street*
*P.O. Box 835*
*Renton*
*(206) 227-RAIL or (800) 876-RAIL (7245)*
*$$$$$*

"All aboard!" is the call for this unique dining experience. The Spirit of Washington Dinner Train serves up gourmet cuisine, scrumptious desserts, and award-winning wines. The train speeds along as you dine in a luxurious, vintage rail car. The trip is three-and-a half hours along a scenic route where you can enjoy views of Lake Washington, the Olympic Mountains, the Seattle skyline and Mount Rainier until finally you arrive at the Columbia Winery in Woodinville. Once there, you can sample Northwest wines and take a tour of the winery, before returning to the train.

You do need to make reservations for the Spirit of Washington Dinner Train, so call ahead for information on the menu, times and current rates.

## Victoria Clipper Sunset Cruise

*Pier 69/Alaskan Way*
*Seattle*
*(206) 448-5000*

Nothing says romance like a sunset cruise. If you don't have your own sea vessel, try the Victoria Clipper Sunset Cruises. The ships run July and August, sailing out to Bainbridge Island and back. Food and beverages are available on the ship. The views of Seattle and the romantic outside decks are wonderful. There are also live jazz cruises, which blend fine music and scenery together.

All rates and dates are subject to change, so call ahead for information about the cruises.

## Waterfront Streetcar

*Pier 70 (Broad and Alaskan Way)*
*5th & Jackson/International District*
*(206) 553-3000 (Metro schedule and fare information-24-hour service)*

You'll step back in time when you choose this alternative form of transportation for your day or evening activities. The Waterfront Streetcar is an old-fashioned trolley that runs all the way from Pier 70, at Broad Street, to the International District. It makes stops at the Pike Place Market, the waterfront piers and Pioneer Square, among others. There are dozens of eating and shopping options along the route.

The streetcar runs every day, but there are different hours for winter (September-February) and summer runs. Generally, the trolley operates from 7:00 A.M. until 6:00 P.M., with additional runs during the summer until approximately 8:00 P.M. Because the schedule varies, call the Metro info line before you make a date; they will also send you a current schedule of times and fares. Your ticket lets you ride for up to 90 minutes. The fares also vary according to season and time of day; generally plan on a maximum of $1.00 and a low of 75 cents. Compare these rates to cab fare from Pier 56 to Pioneer Square! Besides being economical, the trolley is a fun and different way to explore Seattle. By checking the morning newspaper, you can plan your trip to include a romantic sunset view from the streetcar.

## Woodland Park Zoo

*5500 Phinney Avenue, Seattle*
*(206) 684-4800 (zoo information line)*
*$*

The Woodland Park Zoo is great fun for animal lovers of all ages. If you haven't been to the zoo lately, you don't know what you're missing! This is rated one of the 10 best zoos in the country, and over three-fourths of it has been remodeled to create authentic surroundings for the animals. Exhibits include The Tropical Rainforest, The Northern Trail, The Trail of Vines and Family Farm. If you want to take a picnic, there are tables available, or you can bring along a blanket. There are numerous snack bars with hot dogs, popcorn, cotton candy and all the great "zoo" favorites you loved as a kid. Sharing a cotton candy is a fine American romantic tradition! The Rainforest Cafe is an indoor and outdoor food court, offering a wide range of food. It accepts cash only.

Some of the special events at the zoo include: Endangered Species Month in March, International Migratory Bird Day Walk, Woodland Park ZooTunes in July and August, and the annual Holiday Zoobilee. There are also many other events for zoo members only (if you'd like to join, give the zoo a call). The Woodland Park ZooTunes are quite popular, and are held in the zoo's North Meadow. This annual summer concert series includes rock, folk and jazz performances. Call to receive a complete schedule of groups and dates. Concerts begin at 7:00 P.M., so you can top off a day at the zoo with an evening picnic and outdoor entertainment. For the kids, the zoo offers Woodland Park ZooTunes Jr. where families can enjoy a variety of children's musical and humorous performers.

The hours are 9:30 A.M. to 6:00 P.M. March 15-October 14, and 9:30 A.M. to 4:00 P.M. October 15-March 14. (The gates reopen for the Summer Concerts.) King County residents receive a discount on the zoo admission price.

Stepping Out in Seattle

# Shopping Fun

$S$hopping can be a great excuse to get together with someone you don't know very well. Call that someone special on the phone and say, "I have to buy a new pair of pants, want to come with me?" Now you're spending a casual day together without the pressure of a "real date." You'll talk, walk around and maybe share a meal together. It's a no-pressure situation. If you're already a couple, you probably shop together a lot. Why not try a new mall, or go just to window-shop during the holiday season. It can be an inexpensive way to spend a wet and cold Seattle day.

# Bellevue Square

*Between NE 4th and NE 8th*
*On Bellevue Way*
*(425) 454-8096*

Bellevue Square is home to every store you're looking for, and a few you didn't know existed. With Nordstrom, JC Penney, and The Bon Marché as anchor stores, and specialty shops galore, Bellevue Square is a shopper's dream. Head to Bellevue Square on a cold and wet Saturday. Stroll through the mall, do a little shopping, stop for lunch, and enjoy each other's company. Although shopping is an art in itself, you may feel the need for a little more culture in your life. If so, head upstairs to the regionally acclaimed Bellevue Art Museum. (For more information, see chapter 1, *Cultural Attractions*.) BAM (as it is known to its friends) is located on the third floor and is a real treat. Bellevue Square also hosts the Pacific Northwest Arts and Crafts fair, offers live music during the Christmas season, and trick-or-treating for the kids at Halloween (to name a few events). Walking through the mall under the white lights, and Christmas caroling, can be very romantic. So, call that someone special and head to Bellevue Square.

# The Broadway Market

*401 Broadway E*
*Seattle*
*(206) 322-1610*

A Broadway version of Bellevue Square and The Pike Place Market, the Broadway Market shopping center is unique in our area. Granted, it has all the usual mall amenities such as stores and food, but it also has a movie theater, a gallery, a half-price ticket outlet, and numerous funky stands. Seattle Floral is on the corner, if you want to buy a pretty bouquet or a single stunning blossom. The Broadway Market is a great place to spend time wandering around before a movie, or just browsing anytime. The hours are from 10:00 A.M. to 9:00 P.M. Monday through Saturday, and from 12:00 noon to 6:00 P.M. Sunday.

# Chandler's Cove

*901 Fairview Avenue N*
*On Lake Union/Seattle*

Before, or after, a delicious meal, you should explore Chandler's Cove. This little cluster of specialty shops is located right on the water, and offers everything from clothing to crystals to cookware. This can be an especially handy option while waiting for your table reservation, or for your name to come up at Cucina! Cucina! which does not take reservations. It's also a pleasant way to end a romantic stroll along the lake. If you love sweets, stop in for a dessert or espresso at City Sweets, or pick up a picnic at the deli. A Versateller is also located in Chandler's Cove, just in case.

## DOWNTOWN SEATTLE RETAIL

## Downtown Seattle

Downtown Seattle retail stores have experienced a rebirth and are an ideal shopping destination. Nordstrom and The Bon Marché are located right in the center of things. Then there are numerous retail attractions for you to explore. Some stores not to be missed include: FAO Schwartz and The Disney Store (for the kid in you), Nike Town (for the athlete in you), the Levi's Store (for the "casual" you) and REI* (for the rock climber in you). The city is spending money on new parking structures and new retail stores, to help make the downtown area a fun stop for shoppers. Stop for a bite to eat at any one of the colorful restaurants situated in the area. A few suggested spots are: Palomino, Planet Hollywood or ObaChine. (See chapter 2, *Restaurants*, for more information and suggestions.)

*Note: REI is not located right downtown. However, it isn't far from the hustle and bustle of central downtown. It's located at 222 Yale Avenue North (phone (206) 223-1944), and has a World Wrapps restaurant inside the store (phone (206) 223-0222). The biggest attraction at REI is the climbing rock, which stands three stories high and is open to the public.

# Gilman Village

*317 NW Gilman Village Boulevard*
*Issaquah (I-90 exit #17, bear right)*
*(425) 462-0594*

Gilman Village is a destination shopping "center" with a rustic theme. It's easy to spend the better part of a day exploring the various shops. All the stores range from funky to boutique; this is *not* your average strip mall. Couples and friends can be found buying a balloon from the Red Balloon Company, a keepsake of dried flowers, a favorite book, or any number of unique gifts. The stores and restaurants in Gilman Village open at 10:00 on weekdays and Saturdays, 11:00 A.M. on Sunday, and close around 6:00 P.M. on weekdays and Saturdays, 5:00 P.M. on Sunday.

Here are some spots for a late lunch or snack, and a great little Italian restaurant, all within the boundaries of the Village:

The Snow Goose Cafe (phone (425) 391-4671) is a quaint farmlike restaurant with an outdoor deck. You can enjoy salads and sandwiches, and beer, wine or espresso. The Snow Goose Cafe is connected to Made in Washington, a fun store filled with Washington State gifts and products. The Snow Goose accepts Visa, Mastercard and personal checks. The hours are 8:00 A.M. to 5:00 P.M.; during the summer they are open until 8:00 P.M. on Thursday nights. Entrée prices: $

Also try The Art House Cafe, Tantalus Greek Restaurant, Wildfire Ranch BBQ and Sweet Addition (which has desserts, candy and an ice-cream parlor).

Nicolino Ristorante Italiano (phone (425) 391-8077) remains open later than the rest of Gilman Village. Dinner is served from 5:00 P.M. to 10:00 P.M. and seating is first come, first served. Dress is casual. The decor is black-and-white checkered floors with small tables and marble tabletops. An Italian fresco adorns the wall. Adding to the authentic Italian feel is the voice of an Italian tenor on tape in the background. There's also a small patio with tables around a fountain. This wonderful little restaurant, whose chef is from Italy, is becoming very popular with Eastsiders. Also open for lunch, Nicolino Ristorante Italiano accepts Visa, Mastercard and personal checks. Entrée prices: $$

# The Pike Place Market

*Upper level: First & Pike*
*Lower level: Western & Pike*
*Downtown Seattle/Waterfront*
*(206) 682-7453*

The Pike Place Market is a great place to spend a morning or an entire day. The stands themselves close down between 5:00 and 6:00 P.M., but many of the restaurants are open later. The outdoor market first opened in 1907 and includes fish stands and vendors offering fresh fruits and vegetables and various Northwest arts and crafts. If it's food you're looking for, the market has Asian, Turkish, Greek, Italian, Malaysian, Mexican, and Russian (to name only a few). The Sound View Cafe offers one of the best views in the city, looking out over the Puget Sound toward Alki Point. For dessert, try one of the ice cream or frozen yogurt shops, many of which also serve espresso. Stop by the information booth to obtain a complete listing of restaurants in the Market.

People-watching is perhaps one of the best things about the Market. Talking about the interesting people you see is one way to ease the awkwardness of a first date. The Market is most lively during the warm, summer months; however the tourist crowds are larger then as well. If you don't like crowds, off-season, misty days have a whole different feel, and are more relaxed. The various street and sidewalk musicians provide a touch of "culture;" you'll hear everything from classical to folk, and lots in between.

A cash machine is located at the information booth in front of the fish market, near the clock. On busy days, get your cash before you arrive; lines can be long or the machine empty. How much money you spend is entirely up to where you go and what you eat or buy.

# University Village Shopping Center

*2673 NE University Village*
*Seattle*
*(206) 523-0622*

University Village has undergone an extensive remodel, and is home to great shops such as Eddie Bauer, Barnes & Noble, Starbucks Coffee, Pasta & Co., and The Gap. The shopping center is a combination of brick buildings, patios, and hanging flowers. One of the few outdoor malls, this is a wonderful place to spend a warm summer evening. You and a friend can wander along, enjoying the shops and the atmosphere of this quaint shopping spot. Starbucks Coffee presents free live jazz concerts on Friday and Saturday evenings after 8:00 P.M. There is also a great little Italian restaurant called Ristorante Piatti. It is located at 2800 NE University Village Mall (206) 524-9088.

## Westlake Center

*1605 Fifth Avenue*
*Downtown Seattle*
*(206) 467-1600*

Shopping can be a great way to spend time together, even if it's just window-shopping. One of the more interesting places for this is the Westlake Center in downtown Seattle. For those who love the art of shopping, this place is like a museum! There are more than 80 specialty stores, a food court and an outdoor plaza. You can try on clothes and hats, or check out the Northwest Tribal Art store or the Museum of Flight store. Or people-watch, or browse for books. If things get dull, take a ride on the Monorail (located just outside) to Seattle Center.

The food court, called the Pacific Picnic, offers a variety of food options from hot dogs to Turkish specialties. When the weather is nice, you can listen to one of the numerous bands perform in the plaza outside. Parking is available in the Westlake Center Parking Garage on Olive Way, between Fourth and Fifth Avenues.

The Westlake Center's hours change with the seasons. Winter hours: Monday through Friday 9:30 A.M. to 8:00 P.M., Saturday 9:30 A.M. to 7:00 P.M., and Sunday 11:00 A.M. to 6:00 P.M. Summer hours: Monday through Friday 9:30 A.M. to 9:00 P.M., Saturday 9:30 A.M. to 7:00 P.M., and Sunday 11:00 A.M. to 6:00 P.M. Winter hours last from December 27 to May 31 and summer hours are from June 1 to November 24. Shop 'til you drop!

# NOTEWORTHY NEIGHBORHOODS

There are many wonderful neighborhoods in the Greater Seattle Area to explore. Here are a few with a lot to offer. This is by no means a complete list (and don't rule out your own special neighborhood), but these are some good ones to visit.

## Alki Strip

The Alki Strip runs along Puget Sound and reminds you of a California beach town, without the smog, traffic and blistering heat. Alki Way, which used to be full of small beach homes, is now loaded with beautiful new beachfront condos. As you drive along the strip, enjoy breathtaking views over the Sound looking towards Seattle or out towards the San Juan Islands. A paved path follows the strip, so you can walk, jog, bike or roller-blade. Alki can get crowded on those rare, sunny Saturdays in Seattle, so you might want to get an early start. Actually, I think a stroll on the beach on a cloudy day can be very romantic.

The restaurants of Alki start at 57th and run through 63rd, all on Alki Way and all with views of Puget Sound. Here are some you should check out. The Alki Bakery and Alki Cafe make great breakfast or lunch spots. Boca serves up Mediterranean specialties. Try their "Jerk BBQ" (a Jamaican blend of seasonings). This place is fun! The Cherry Blossom Teriyaki has takeout and outdoor seating. The Point Grille has outdoor seating and serves a wide variety of food. Pegasus is the place for pizza, pasta and salads and also has outdoor seating. Spud Fish and Chip is THE place for fish and chips. Get an order, then take it across the street and have a beach picnic. There are many other spots to try with a friend or date, so put on your sunscreen and head for the beach!

## Broadway

The great thing about Seattle is the diversity of people who live and work here. Broadway is one of those places where all kinds of people, food and cultures are expressed. This makes for a great place to go with a friend because the many Broadway offerings suit every mood and taste. You can park the car at one end of the strip, then wander along until you find something of interest. Here are a few spots which are especially popular. They are listed from north to south as you walk down Broadway.

Deluxe Bar & Grille (625 Broadway E), Starbucks Coffee (516), La Cocina & Cantina (432), Dilettante Chocolates (416), The Broadway Market (401), Broadway New American Grill (314), Angel's Thai Cuisine (235), Charlie's (217) and Espresso Roma (202). This list is by no means complete, but it is a good place to start. Remember, just exploring a neighborhood is fun; you don't need to have a plan every time you go out with a friend.

## Kirkland Waterfront

*Kirkland Chamber of Commerce*
*(425) 822-7066*

The Kirkland Waterfront is a beautiful neighborhood stretching along Lake Washington. The main strip runs along Lake Washington Boulevard and is between 5th Avenue and Central Way. There is parking on the street, and parking lots at the corner of Lake Washington Boulevard and Central Way. Kirkland is a wonderful place to spend a summer evening, especially if you aren't sure what you want for dinner. You can stroll along picturesque Lake Washington, while looking for a restaurant. The shops include: antiques, clothes, ice cream, flowers, jewelers, art galleries and coffee shops and more. There is also a great pool hall, The Shark Billiard, on Central Avenue.

Kirkland also offers great restaurants: Anthony's Home Port, Calabria, The Crabcracker, Cucina! Presto!, Hector's, JJJ Cafe, Kirkland Roaster & Ale House, Portofino, and World Wrapps. (This is not a complete list, but a good place to start.) Kirkland also invites you to join in *Taste! Kirkland*, a smaller version of *Bite of Seattle* street festival. It's a great place to try many of Kirkland's restaurants all at once. The festival also hosts a Beach to Bay Run, Magnificent Mutt Parade and a kids bike parade. *Taste! Kirkland* takes place during September. Call the Chamber of Commerce for details.

For a bit of culture, try Kirkland's Jazz Night, the first Wednesday of the month in Downtown Kirkland. (Call the Chamber for more information). If you prefer visual art to music, join the monthly Gallery Walk on the second Thursday. The galleries of Kirkland invite you to learn more about the local art and artists. The Art Walk is from 6:00 P.M. to 9:00 P.M. and has covered free parking at the Kirkland Library.

## Madison Park

Madison Park runs along East Madison between 40th and 43rd. You can park on the street and wander the strip. There's a great view of Lake Washington at the end of East Madison. This quiet neighborhood is always full of local residents, many walking their dogs. It's a peaceful place to spend an afternoon. For your convenience, Madison Park has a Versateller at the corner of 41st and E Madison.

Area restaurants include: Bistro & Bites (lunch), Bruegger's Bagels, Cactus, Madison Park Bakery, Mad Pizza, Manca's, Mangoes Thai, and Sorella's. For dessert, try Scoop de jour Ice Creamery, a very popular spot during the summer. Espresso coffee can be found at Starbucks or Tully's, and The Attic and The Red Onion Tavern are fun bars if you're in the mood for a drink.

## Redmond

*Redmond Chamber of Commerce*
*(425) 885-4014*

With high-tech companies such as Microsoft headquartered in Redmond, the city has grown quite a bit over the past few years. The Chamber of Commerce is excited to welcome Redmond Town Center, a combination of shopping, businesses, movie theaters and restaurants. Although the downtown is growing, the surrounding beauty of the area will remain undisturbed. Marymoor Park still provides green grass, trees and a taste of nature.

Redmond is full of great outing ideas, but here are a few you might try. Take a bicycle ride through Marymoor Park, picnic at the windmill and tour the Marymoor Museum. Sample brews and listen to live jazz Thursday and Friday nights at the Redmond Brewing Company. On a dreary, rainy day you can catch a flick at the Bella Bottega Cinemas. Take a stroll through the Redmond Saturday Market, on Leary Way, or browse the Golden Days antique store in town. Couples can enjoy a romantic weekend of pampering at the Cottage Creek Inn Bed & Breakfast.

Shopping is a great way to spend time together, and Redmond is proud to show off the new Redmond Town Center (425) 867-0808. This beautiful mall contains a variety of upscale stores and restaurants. Among the shops are Ann Taylor, Border's Books, Eddie Bauer, The Gap, Limited Express, Nine West and Victoria's Secret. Restaurants include Asia Grille, Canyon Cafe, Cucina! Cucina! and Starbucks. There is also a Cineplex Odeon Theater for your movie pleasure. This center will definitely be a popular spot for friends, families and dates.

# Chapter Five

# Indoor & Outdoor Play

*T*here seems to be an unlimited number of ways to play in the Puget Sound region. For starters, our list includes ideas for both indoor and outdoor recreation, with a sampling of activities ranging from bowling to rock-climbing. If you have a competitive spirit, you soon learn what happens when the gauntlet is down and the challenge begins in such arenas as the tennis court or billiards hall. This is especially helpful in assessing the likelihood that the relationship will move successfully into more cooperative stages. But if competition's not your thing, dancing and canoeing are popular noncompetitive activities for lovers and friends.

## BILLIARDS

### Belltown Billiards

*90 Blanchard Street*
*Seattle*
*(206) 448-6779*
*21 and over (valid identification required)*
*$-$$*

The Belltown Billiards and Restaurant is a full-service restaurant, full bar and billiards hall. The restaurant serves delicious Italian cuisine, while the bar offers a large selection of Northwest wines and microbrews. The atmosphere is metropolitan, with live music, including jazz and popular local acts, adding flair. This isn't your typical smoky pool dive; this is a classy joint! Belltown was voted one of the "Top Five Billiard Rooms in the Country" by Billiards Digest. It makes a great date destination. You can have drinks and a delicious dinner, then listen to live jazz, and indulge your competitive spirit with a game of pool.

If Italian food doesn't fit your mood, try the Queen City Grille, right above Belltown Billiards. On the corner of Blanchard and First, this cozy, casual little spot serves up fresh fish. It's a great dinner spot before a few games of pool.

### Jillian's Billiard Club and Cafe

*731 Westlake N*
*Just off SW Lake Union*
*(206) 223-0300*
*21 and over (valid identification required)*
*$-$$*

You don't have to be an expert pool player to enjoy a night at Jillian's. This pool hall, bar and restaurant is a great place for friends and couples. You can kick back and play a couple of games of pool, and enjoy appetizers, pizza, burgers, and the like, while you are relaxing. A main feature of this upscale billiard parlor (which covers two floors) is the original bar from the old Algonquin Hotel in New York City. The general decor complements the elegant bar, with green carpet, brass and mahogany trimmings throughout. The age of the crowd ranges from early twenties to thirty-plus. There is plenty of background music and conversation, but it never gets so loud you can't hear each other.

Dress is casual to after-work clothes, depending on the time and the night. There is a dress code, however, so no baseball caps, cut-off shorts or jeans with holes. Jillian's is open until 2:00 A.M. during the week, and until 4:00 A.M. on weekends. Nonsmoking tables are available on request. Visa and Mastercard accepted, but no checks.

## 2-11 Billiard Club

*2304 Second Avenue*
*Downtown Seattle*
*(206) 443-1211*
*$-$$*

Billiards has made a comeback in the past few years. The 2-11 Billiard Club is a popular hangout for both novices and experts. The atmosphere looks as if you'd expect: there is nothing pretentious or stuffy about this pool hall. The age range of the players is anywhere from twenty-one to sixty-plus, and there is a definite sense of camaraderie.

The 2-11 club attracts a college crowd on the weekends, and an older, regular crowd during the week. This is a great way to enjoy a casual evening, playing pool, drinking beer and watching the other games. The 2-11 is open Monday through Saturday from 11:00 A.M. to 1:30 A.M., and from 3:00 P.M. to 11:00 P.M. on Sundays. Rack 'em up!

## BOWLING

A night of bowling can be a terrific evening, whether or not you and your date know much about the game. In most bowling alleys, you can also opt for video games or shoot some pool. All this costs less than a movie, and you can have fun and talk and just generally enjoy each other's company. There are vending machines available, plus a restaurant and a lounge. Bowling is a great physical activity to participate in with a friend or that someone special. With the rapid extinction of bowling lanes in our area, you might want to put this one on your "do it soon" list.

# Imperial Lanes

*2101 22nd Avenue*
*Seattle*
*(206) 325-2525*
*$*

Imperial Lanes is open 24 hours a day, which makes it a great late-night date spot. There are 24 lanes, and food is served at the Satellite Sports Pub & Eatery. During the summer months there are plenty of lanes available, but lane availability is limited in the fall and winter due to bowling leagues. Imperial Lanes hosts "Cosmic Bowl" on Friday and Saturday evenings, complete with strobe lights, loud music and a fog machine. "Cosmic Bowl" makes bowling quite an experience!

# Kenmore 50 Lanes

*7638 NE Bothell Way*
*Bothell*
*(425)486-5555*
*$*

Open 24 hours, this popular bowling establishment has no light show and no smoke, but they do offer a good time and a good lane to bowl on. If you're serious about bowling, or you think loud music distracts you from your game, you will definitely like Kenmore Lanes. They also have video games, a restaurant, lounge and snack vending machines. The cost to bowl varies slightly with the time of day or night.

# Skyway Park Bowl

*11819 Renton Avenue*
*South Seattle*
*(206) 772-1220*
*$*

Skyway Park Bowl offers much more than just bowling. There's Bumber Bowling for the kids, Karaoke in the lounge, a card room, a pro shop and miniature golf. This is also the home of Seattle's newest state-of-the-art miniature golf course. Obviously, the atmosphere is fun and playful. You could spend the whole day deciding what to do. Just make sure you come ready to play! The hours of operation are 8:00 A.M. to 2:00 A.M.

# Sunvilla Bowling Lanes

*3080 148th SE*
*Eastgate Shopping Center (behind Safeway)*
*Off I-90 at 150th Street Exit, Bellevue*
*(425) 455-8155*
*$*

Sunvilla has 32 lanes and Bumber Bowling for kids. Weekend events here are lots of fun, and include "Rock & Bowl" on Friday nights, with loud music, "Moonlight Bowling" on Saturday nights, where you can win cash prizes but you must be eighteen, and "Country Bowl" on Sunday nights, featuring, you guessed it, country music. There is a restaurant and lounge, as well as vending machines. The Fun Zone is a game room with redemption games, video games and crane games. Sunvilla is open from 9:00 A.M. to 11:00 P.M. Sunday through Thursday; from 9:00 A.M. to 2:00 A.M. Friday and Saturday.

# Totem Bowl

*13033 NE 70th Place*
*(Bridle Trails Shopping Center)*
*Kirkland*
*(425) 827-0785*
*$*

Totem Bowl has video games and a restaurant, lounge and vending machines. There's "X-Bowl" every Friday and Saturday night, with disco lights, glow-in-the-dark pins, and pulsating rhythms by the in-house DJ. There is also a "Sunday Morning Special," where all games before noon are discounted. Open from 9:00 A.M. to 2:00 A.M. daily.

## DANCING

# The Washington Dance Club

*1017 Stewart Street*
*Corner of Stewart and Boren*
*(206) 628-8939*
*$*

The Washington Dance Club offers lessons, and is open to the public two evenings a week. Admission is very reasonable for an evening of ballroom, swing and Latin dancing. Nonalcoholic refreshments are served. On Friday nights, there is a dance workshop from 8:00 to 9:00 P.M., and then a dance from 9:00 to 11:30 P.M. The workshops change weekly, so call ahead to find out what type of dance is being taught. On Sunday nights, the public dancing is from 7:00 until 9:00 P.M.

Although ballroom dancing may appear to be a lost art, the Washington Dance Club offers the following suggestions of other local places to enjoy an evening on the dance floor:

**Beso Del Sol** (4468 Stone Way N; (206) 547-8087) provides Salsa/Disco Music on a regular basis. **The Red Lion Hotel at Sea-Tac** (18740 Pacific Highway S; (206) 246-8600 and **Bellevue** (300 112th SE; (425) 455-1300) has ballroom and/or swing dances. Call for details. **The Four Seasons Olympic Hotel** holds dancing in the **Garden Court** (411 University Street; (206) 621-1700). **The Seattle Center** (206) 684-8582; (206) 684-7200 also holds ballroom and square dancing regularly.

For more dancing opportunities, see Chapter 8, *Dancing, Music & Club-Hopping.*

## HORSE RACING

## Emerald Downs

*2300 Emerald Downs Drive*
*Auburn*
*(253) 288-7000*
*$*

Enjoy a day of thoroughbred racing with someone special. You'll get a rush screaming for your horse as it gallops around the track. The beautifully landscaped track is a great place to enjoy a summer afternoon together. The park also has a restaurant and lounge. Races run Thursday through Sunday, March through September. There are also special events such as live concerts and family Sundays during the summer months. Call Emerald Downs directly for more information.

## BICYCLING & OUTDOOR ACTIVITIES

## Gregg's Greenlake Cycle Inc.

*7007 Woodlawn NE*
*Green Lake*
*(206) 523-1822*
*$*

Whether you are seriously into sports or just in the mood for a little exercise, Green Lake is the primo urban destination for a variety of outdoor athletic activities. Gregg's Greenlake Cycle Inc. rents bikes, roller skates and roller blades by the hour. You can race around the lake, or take a leisurely stroll and enjoy the scenery. Either way, you get to enjoy being outdoors, being together, and watching the interesting "traffic" around the lake. Gregg's requires a Washington State driver's license, so be prepared. Gregg's is open for rentals from 9:30 A.M. to 7:30 P.M. every day. Renting outdoor equipment is dependent on the weather, so check the forecast before making this date! Check out Seattle's Best Coffee (6850 E Green Lake Way N) for an iced coffee or coffee milkshake.

*Note:* Paddleboats are available for rent through the concessionaire at the Green Lake Boathouse from April 1 to September 30 (206) 527-0171.

## The Mountaineers Club

*300 Third Avenue W*
*Lower Queen Anne*
*(206) 284-6310 (Club Office)*
*(206) 284-8484 (Club Sign-up)*

The Mountaineers Club offers great opportunities to couples and singles who live in the Northwest because they love the outdoors. There's an extremely active singles group, but you are also welcome to bring a date along to any of the many activities. (Note: if you are a steady couple, you will both be required to join after a few times. The single fee is $39). The club puts on dances where you don't need to be, or even know, a member.

By joining the club, you can enjoy a broad range of guided activities: hiking, canoeing, folk dance, climbing, bicycling, outdoor photography, sailing, snowshoeing, and more. As a member, you can invite a guest to any of the various events. How many dates have you taken snowshoeing? The club provides introductory to advanced opportunities for you and a friend, or spouse.

For more information on joining the Mountaineers, call the office from 8:30 A.M. to 6:30 P.M. Monday through Friday. There is a bookstore which is open from 10:00 A.M. to 6:30 P.M., and information meetings at 7:30 P.M. on the first Wednesday of every month.

# ICE-SKATING & ROLLER-SKATING

## Highland Ice Arena

*18005 Aurora Avenue N*
*North Seattle/Shoreline*
*(206) 546-2431*
*$*

Take a friend or date ice-skating any time of the year at the Highland Ice Arena. Dress in warm clothes and slowly circle the rink, or make this a sporting event and go for the Gold. The rink is open year round, but public skating hours change regularly due hockey schedules, lessons etc. Public sessions are daily, but call ahead for the hours open. Professional fitting and skate sharpening is available, and there are snack machines in the lobby.

## Lynnwood's Sno-King Ice Arena

*19803 68th Avenue W*
*Lynnwood/Edmonds border*
*(425) 775-7511*
*$*

The newly remodeled Sno-King offers a wide variety of skating sessions: public "open" skate times, lessons, "sticks and pucks," and figure-skating competitions. It's best to call the information number before you make your plans, as sessions do change frequently. They are open seven days a week, all year, for your skating enjoyment. There is a snack bar to stop and fuel up at. Try the hot chocolate to take the chill off.

# Ronald McDonald House Ice Rink

*The Seattle Center*
*Winter holiday season only*
*(206) 684-7200 (Seattle Center Info. Line)*

For the skating schedule of this popular outdoor seasonal rink, call the Seattle Center information number. The proceeds from your admission ticket go to Ronald McDonald House, so you can feel good about helping a worthy cause while having a good time. Enjoy the magic of the holidays by taking the Monorail downtown to look at all the sparkling Christmas lights. The rink is only open during Winterfest at the Seattle Center.

# Skate King

*2301 140th*
*Bellevue*
*(425) 641-2046*
*$*

If ice is a little too cold for your taste, try roller-skating or roller-blading. This is a great way to spend a rainy day and it's good cardiovascular activity as well. Anyone who was a teenager in the '80s will remember when roller-skating made its big comeback. Take your date down Memory Lane as you skate hand-in-hand to the "Snow-Ball" skate. Skate King also hosts Tiny Tots, Christian Music Skate Night, and R & B Skate Night. There is also a snack bar to share one coke with two straws! Skate King accepts cash only.

# KAYAK & CANOE RENTALS

An outdoor adventure can make for a great Northwest-style date. Why not rent a canoe or kayak? The listings below rent canoes, kayaks and double kayaks by the hour. Paddling around Lake Union any time of day is scenic and interesting. At sunset, the lake can be very romantic. Bring a picnic and the day will be complete. You can also dock at one of the popular lakeside restaurants for a beverage or a bite to eat.

## Agua Verde Paddle Club

*1303 NE Boat Street*
*(206) 545-8570*
*$*

Agua Verde's staff will help you get your sea legs before you head out on the lake. Hourly kayak rentals on Portage Bay, Lake Union. Open from 9:00 A.M. to 9:00 P.M. daily.

## Northwest Outdoor Center

*2100 Westlake N*
*West side of Lake Union*
*(206) 281-9694*
*$*

Northwest Outdoor will give you any advice and instructions necessary before you head out, and they supply flotation devices. Rental hours are Monday through Friday, 10:00 A.M. to 8:00 P.M.; Saturday and Sunday, 9:00 A.M. to 6:00 P.M.

## Paddle Seattle

*2100 Westlake Avenue N*
*Seattle*
*(206) 281-9694*
*$*

Enjoy spectacular views from your kayak, rented from Paddle Seattle. Kayaks are available for one, two and three people. The hours are from 10:00 A.M. to 8:00 P.M. Monday through Friday and from 9:00 A.M. to 6:00 P.M. Saturday and Sunday.

## UW Canoe Rentals

*SE corner Husky Stadium Lot (off Montlake Boulevard)*
*University of Washington campus*
*(206) 543-2100*
*Must be 18 and older*
*$-$$ (Hourly rates)*

A canoe for two can be sweetly romantic, just plain fun, or a bit of both. The University of Washington rents canoes, and it's an easy paddle to and around the Arboretum's waterways. Pack a picnic supper and go at sunset, or spend a sunny Saturday playing in the water. The boats must be in by 8:30 P.M., but that still gives you time for dinner under a tree at water's edge. You need a valid driver's license to rent a canoe, so be sure to bring one along. The UW requires, and provides, flotation devices. Canoes are rented from the Waterfront Activity Center, located below Husky Stadium (enter through the West Plaza entrance). There are no reservations, so on a nice day, better be there early. The Waterfront Activity Center is open weekdays from February 8 to October 31st. Hours are 10:00 A.M. to 8:30 P.M. weekdays and weekends from 9:00 A.M. to 8:30 P.M. UW staff and students get a discount. Bon voyage!

## SEATTLE SPORTING EVENTS

Seattle's sport teams are well-loved and supported by the whole community. Taking a friend to a sporting event makes a great date. Here is a list of the teams and phone numbers to call for tickets and information:

**Mariners Baseball** *(206) 628-3555*
**Sonics Basketball** *(206) 281-5850*
**Husky Football** *(206) 543-2200*
**Seahawks Football** *(425) 827-9766*
**Thunderbirds Hockey** *(206) 448-7825*
**SeaDogs Soccer** *(206) 282-3647*

# VIDEO ARCADES

The meaning of the term "video arcade" has changed so much over the years. At one time, an arcade meant a few pinball machines Then it meant standard video games. Today, it involves virtual reality games. Seattle has its fair share of arcades, but here are the "Best of the Best" for you to explore.

## Entros

*823 Yale Avenue N*
*Seattle*
*(206) 624-0057*
*$-$$*

Entros is an intelligent amusement park located near Lake Union. With, engaging, challenging and entertaining games, it has also been recognized for its creative and delicious cuisine. The Entros World Grille offers dishes from around the world, and beer, wine and spirits.

Entros is open from 5:30 P.M. to closing (when everyone goes home), Tuesday through Saturday, and from 5:00 P.M. to 10:30 P.M. Sunday.

## GameWorks

*7th & Pike*
*Meridian Complex*
*Seattle*
*(206) 283-4263*
*$$*

GameWorks is more then a video arcade; it is an upscale venue with an Internet Cafe, brew pub, pizza parlor and Starbucks Coffee. Although teenagers love it, after 8:00 P.M. you must be 18 and over, unless escorted by an adult. At the door you buy a card (approximately $20) that enables you to play all the games in the house. No coins or tokens are used in the arcade. If you want to log onto the Internet, you can join a GameWorks club.

GameWorks hours of operation are: 10:00 A.M. to 12:30 A.M.

Monday through Thursday, 10:00 A.M. to 1:30 A.M. Friday and Saturday, and 11:00 A.M. to 11:00 P.M. Sunday.

## Jazwieck's Golf & Train

*7828 Broadway*
*Everett*
*(425) 355-5646*
*$*

Miniature golf makes a great outing, and it's a great way to get to know each other. After all, miniature golf isn't what you'd call a "fast-paced game." In fact, it takes at least an hour and you can talk while you wait to golf. Jazwieck's offers an 18-hole lighted miniature golf course with train rides on a scenic route. The park is outside, so you can enjoy the trees and beauty of the Pacific Northwest. The train is more for the enjoyment of children, but if your friend or date has kids, bring them along!

The park is open April through September or October (depending on weather conditions). The summer hours are from 12:00 noon to 10:00 P.M. In the fall, winter and spring months, the hours are from 12:00 noon to approximately 6:00 P.M. (closing hours vary).

## Seattle Funplex

*1541 15th Avenue W*
*Seattle*
*(206) 285-7842*
*$*

The Seattle Funplex is an indoor amusement park, perfect for those rainy days in Seattle. Take a friend or date who loves to play, and spend the afternoon having pure, unadulterated fun! The Seattle Funplex has an 18-hole miniature golf course, hard and softball batting cages, laser tag, video games, bumper cars, and a full-service snack bar. There is also a photo booth for you and your sweetie to take a black and white picture in. Nothing makes a more romantic keepsake than a classic photo booth picture!

Admission is free Sunday through Thursday, and there is a

small cover charge after 9:00 P.M. and on weekends. All games are individually priced, so bring those quarters! The Seattle Funplex summer hours are 11:00 A.M. to 12:00 midnight Sunday through Friday, and from 10:00 A.M. to 12:00 midnight Saturday. Regular hours are shorter, so call the Funplex ahead of time to check on current hours.

## Zone's

*2207 Bel-Red Road*
*Bellevue/Redmond border*
*(425) 746-9411*

Zone's is an indoor amusement park for all ages. The giant game room includes miniature golf, video games, pool tables, batting cages, air hockey. . .you get the picture! The miniature golf features a Pacific Northwest theme: the Pike Place Market, a ferry boat, and Microsoft, to name a few! No matter what your age, you'll have fun here. Though Zone's can be loud, and often crowded, you'll be so busy with the games and the surroundings, you won't mind.

Besides a great miniature golf course, Zone's has batting cages and video games. Zone's also has a cafeteria stocked with hot dogs, pizza, soft drinks and espresso. The hours are from 11:00 A.M. to 10:00 P.M., Monday through Thursday, from 11:00 A.M. to 12:00 A.M. on Friday and Saturday, and from 11:00 A.M. to 8:00 P.M. on Sunday.

*Chapter 6*

# Coffeehouses, Brewpubs & Wine Tours

*S*ince Seattle is known around the country as the land of lattes, microbrews, "Grunge Rock," and Mount Rainier, it seems only fitting that this chapter be included in the book. Coffeehouses are great places go with friends or a date. They are usually quiet and you can sit, drink your coffee, and talk for hours without being asked to leave. Brewpubs and Microbreweries are relatively new concepts, but they provide tons of entertainment for friends and couples. They are generally loud, casual and lively. You are sure to find great beer, but often a limited menu. Taking a tour is always fun. Wine tours and wineries are a sophisticated choice for a date or get-together.

## COFFEEHOUSES

# B & O Espresso

*204 Belmont E*
*Seattle*
*(206) 322-5028*

The atmosphere in the B & O is funky and fun. Each table has an oil lamp and a vase full of flowers. The room is dim, with mirrors reflecting the soft candlelight. The walls are covered with interesting art. Besides the delicious coffee drinks, the B & O has desserts to die for. Try a heavenly piece of cake or pie. The crowd is interesting and people-watching is always a lot of fun.

# The Bookstore

*Alexis Hotel*
*1007 First Avenue*
*Downtown Seattle*
*(206) 624-4844*
*$*

The Bookstore is a bar, coffee shop and bookstore. What a combination! The walls are decorated with books, including a large selection of cookbooks, which are for sale. Newspapers are also available to read while you sip your drink or espresso. The menu includes salads, burgers and sandwiches—mostly light items. Starbucks and Seattle's Best Coffee are served, along with wine, beer and mixed drinks.

The atmosphere is upscale, with a little bit of "soho" mixed in. There is soft music playing, but the majority of the low-key background noise comes from conversation. A thirty-plus crowd makes up the majority of the clientele. Smoking is allowed, but there is no designated section available. Parking can be found either in the Alexis Hotel parking garage, or on the street.

The Bookstore is open from 11:30 A.M., until 2:00 A.M., making this an ideal place to drop in after a show. The Bookstore takes major credit cards and checks.

# Dilettante Chocolates

*416 Broadway E*
*Capitol Hill/Seattle*
*(206) 329-6463*

Don't let the name throw you, Dilettante Chocolates is a great coffeehouse. The mood is very romantic, with dim lights and mirrored walls. The tables are close together and the ambiance is intimate. Enjoy your cup of espresso with a bowl of vanilla ice cream, featuring Dilettante's own hot fudge topping drizzled on top. You and your date can share the dessert; one spoon plus two people always equals romance!

# Espresso Roma, Broadway

*202 Broadway E*
*Seattle*
*(206) 324-1866*
*$*

This coffee shop is the perfect place to sit and carry on a quiet conversation. The crowd is typically twenty and over, and is generally an intellectual and artistic group. The tables seat two or three, so a couple can enjoy a little privacy. The walls are decorated with posters and flyers of cultural events. Espresso Roma is open until 11:00 P.M. or 12:00 A.M., depending on the crowd. They do not take credit cards, or checks: Cash only.

# Espresso Roma, University District

*420 University Avenue*
*University District/Seattle*
*(206) 632-6001*
*$*

Located right on "The Ave" near the University of Washington, Espresso Roma is a great people-watching spot. The cement walls are covered with art, posters and flyers. If you just want to chat over a cup of coffee, there's always a lot to look at and talk about, so conversation comes easily. The pleasant hum of conversation inside serves as the backdrop for the constant moving theater out on the street.

The service is casual: you order at the counter and bus your own table. You can also sit on the outdoor deck, which is situated almost on the sidewalk, so you won't miss any of the activity. The ages of the patrons varies, but the majority are college-age and in their twenties. Espresso Roma is open from 7:00 A.M. to 11:00 P.M. Monday through Friday, from 8:00 A.M. to 11:00 P.M. Saturday, and from 9:00 A.M. to 11:00 P.M. Sunday. They do not take credit cards or checks; cash only, please.

## The Grand Illusion Cinema

*1403 & 1405 NE 50th*
*University District/Seattle*
*(206) 523-3935*

The Grand Illusion is a small movie theater/cafe. This interesting combination makes it a great spot for friends and dates. You can see a movie, then retire to the upstairs cafe for coffee. Sit by the fireplace and warm yourself with conversation and espresso. I have to recommend the Espresso Shake for those warm summer nights. This blend of coffee and ice cream is a wonderful end to an evening.

## Seattle's Best, Starbucks, and Tully's Coffee Chains

*Located all over the Greater Seattle area. Check your Yellow Pages for the addresses and phone numbers.*

You'll find at least one of these three almost anywhere you go, and each one has its own attributes. Seattle's Best on Green Lake, for example, overlooks the park and lake. Tully's in Kirkland is right on the main street and convenient to shopping. The Starbucks on Broadway is a great place for people-watching and late-night conversation. I suggest you just pop into one that looks good to you. All three chains serve a great cup of coffee and provide a nice place to relax.

# BREWPUBS AND ALEHOUSES

Brewpubs and microbreweries originated here in the Pacific Northwest, and there are many to choose from.* Below is a list of the popular brewpubs and alehouses of Seattle. I won't even pretend this list is complete, but they are guaranteed fun places.

*For more information on Brewpubs, check out The Brewpub Explorer of the Pacific Northwest, by Hudson Dodd, Matthew Latterell, Lani MacCormack and Ina Zucker, published by JASI Books. This book gives you detailed information on Brewpubs, Microbreweries and Craft Breweries in Oregon, Washington and British Columbia, Canada, as well as addresses, hours, food, entertainment, directions and more detailed information about the breweries.

## Breweries:

**Big Time Brewery**
*4133 University Way NE*
*Seattle*
*(206) 545-4509*

**Maritime Pacific Brewing Company**
*1514 NW Leary Way*
*Seattle*
*(206) 782-6181*

**Pike Brewing Company**
*1432 Western Avenue*
*Seattle*
*(206) 622-3373*

**Redhook Ale Brewery-The Trolleyman Pub**
*3400 Phinney Avenue N*
*Seattle*
*(206) 548-8000*

**Hale's Ales (Fremont)**
*4301 Leary Way*
*Seattle*
*(206) 782-0737*

**Pacific Brewing Company Limited**
*322 Occidental Avenue S*
*Seattle*
*(206) 621-7002*

**Pyramid Breweries, Inc.**
*91 S Royal Brougham*
*Seattle*
*(206) 682-3377*

**Redhook Ale Brewery-Woodinville**
*14300 NE 145th*
*Woodinville*
*(425) 483-3232*

### Seattle Brewers

530 Holden Street
Seattle
(206) 762-7421

### Seattle Brewing Co./Aviator Ales

14316 NE 203rd Street
Seattle
(206) 938-2476

### West Seattle Brewing Co./California & Alaska Street Brewery

4720 California Avenue SW
Seattle
(206) 487-0717

## Alehouses:

### The Duchess

2827 NE 55th Street
Seattle
(206) 527-8606

### The Greenlake Alehouse

7305 Aurora Avenue N
Green Lake/Seattle
(206) 781-8337

### Kerryman Pub & Restaurant

722 NE 45th Street
University District/Seattle
(206) 545-2960

### Murphy's Pub

1928 N 45th Street
Wallingford/Seattle
(206) 634-2110

### Red Door Alehouse

3401 N Fremont Avenue
Fremont/Seattle
(206) 547-7521

### Woodland Park Pub

6114 Phinney Avenue N
Seattle
(206) 784-3455

# WINE TOURS

Visiting one of the area's local wineries makes for a fun (and often romantic) outing. Located in beautiful Woodinville, both the Columbia Winery and Chateau Ste. Michelle Winery offer tours, wine-tasting, and beautiful grounds.

## Chateau Ste. Michelle Winery

*1411 NE 145th*
*Take Highway 202 /2 mile south of Woodinville to 145th*
*Woodinville*
*(425) 488-1133 or (425) 488-3300*

Spending an afternoon at Chateau Ste. Michelle Winery makes a great date, no matter how long you have known each other. The winery offers tours every half hour. They last about 45 minutes, cost nothing, and are open to all ages (but you must be twenty-one to sample the wine).

The winery also presents popular outdoor concerts and other events in its amphitheater. (Note: it is festival seating.) You can snuggle up on a blanket (bring your own) or you can bring folding chairs. Pack a picnic supper, or buy one from Ste. Michelle (all alcoholic beverages must be purchased from the winery). During the holiday season, caroling and other festive attractions take place indoors.

If you and your companion are athletic, you can ride bikes, or walk, to the winery via the Sammamish River trail, which runs along the west edge of Marymoor Park. Late fall is an especially pleasant time to visit, since the grapes are being pressed and the odor fills the air.

Chateau Ste. Michelle is open from 10:00 A.M. to 6:00 P.M. seven days a week. For tour information, call (425) 488-7733. More information on the Summer Festival can be obtained by calling (425) 488-3300. For tickets to the Summer concerts, call Ticketmaster at (206) 628-0888.

# Columbia Winery

*14030 NE 145th*
*Woodinville*
*(425) 488-2776*

Located only 30 minutes from downtown Seattle, and situated in the beautiful Sammamish Valley, lies Columbia Winery, Washington's first premium winery.

Columbia Winery is romance wrapped up in a Victorian-style mansion. Friends of all ages can sample award-winning wines at the state's largest tasting bar, or sip wine on the deck or verandah and watch hot-air balloons drift by. Tours are available on weekends and upon request during the week. Columbia Winery is also the destination spot for the Spirit of Washington Dinner Train—a fantastic way to enjoy Eastside Seattle from an unusual perspective.

The winery is easy to find; it's right in the heart of the Woodinville tourist district. The adjacent Burke-Gilman Trail is perfect for a summer stroll, cycle, or skate after a stop at the winery. The tasting room and its unique retail store are open every day from 10 A.M. to 7 P.M.

# Chapter 7

# Movie Theaters

$\mathcal{M}$ ovies make great first dates and blind dates, because you don't have to talk for two hours. Then, when the movie is over, you have at least one thing to discuss. Movies also stimulate deeper discussions between good friends. Since the newspaper listings don't go much beyond the current screenings, here is some information about local theaters from the "far-out-funky" to the "trendy-modern" in both the films they show and the theater interior decor. The suggestions below are listed in alphabetical order.

It is standard among movie theaters to take cash only. No checks. No credit cards. The newer theaters have cash machines in the lobbies, but the best advice is, be sure you have a $20 bill in hand before you arrive. Also, movie ticket prices periodically go up. Always call ahead and make sure you know how much current ticket prices are.

Thanks to increasing technology, going to the movies is getting easier and easier! Now you can call one number for information on showtimes, theaters, and even purchase tickets with your credit card over the phone. Movie Phone is brought to you by *Seattle Weekly* and *Eastside Week* and the phone number is (206) 443-FILM (or, (206) 443-4567). Movie Phone is a lot quicker (and cleaner) than searching the newspaper!

# Broadway Market Cinemas

*425 Broadway E*
*In the Broadway Market*
*(206) 323-0231*

This theater is located upstairs in the Broadway Market and features popular movies. The theater validates one hour of parking in the underground parking garage. Catch a movie before or after you shop or eat and drink at the Broadway Market.

# Crest Cinema Center

*16505 Fifth Avenue*
*Corner of NE 165th & 5th NE*
*Ridgecrest*
*(206) 363-6338*

The Crest is a truly inexpensive date spot, because all seats are $2.00, every day! There are also double-bill movies (where you can see two for one ticket) featured. There are five movie theaters. The Crest screens both "intellectual" fare and new, general-audience movies.

# Crossroads Cinemas

*1200 156th NE*
*Behind the Crossroads Mall*
*Bellevue*
*(425) 443-2283*

Crossroads is a newly remodeled cineplex which comprises a total of eight theaters showing first-run movies. Both exterior and interior are ultramodern. There is a cash machine in the lobby, just in case you reach into your pocket and come up short. The theater is near numerous restaurants such as Chili's, BurgerMaster, Black Angus and Cucina Presto, among others. All shows are economy priced before 6:00 P.M. "Monday Night at the Movies" is sponsored by KISW radio where all movies are discounted, except those which are "Starred Attractions."

# Egyptian Theater

*801 Pine*
*Capitol Hill/Seattle*
*(206) 323-4978*

The Egyptian is one large theater, reminiscent of the early days of movie-going. The films run from intellectual to current/popular, but lean toward the artistic. The latté stand right next door is handy for enjoying an espresso while you wait. Bill's Off-Broadway is across the street, if you are in the mood for pizza. (See chapter 2, *Casual Restaurants,* for more information on Bill's.) For a minimum charge, parking is available in the Community College parking lot and the new QFC lot.

# Factoria Cinemas

*3505 128th Avenue SE*
*I-90 at 520/Bellevue*
*(425) 641-9206*

With all the neon lights, you might wonder if you are at a theater or a space ride. Factoria features all current, popular films screened in eight theaters. There are also numerous video games in the lobby. The cineplex is across the street from The Keg restaurant and an assortment of chain and fast food places are close by as well. All shows before 6:00 P.M. are economy-priced.

# Grand Illusion Cinema

*1403 and 1405 NE 50th*
*University District*
*(206) 523-3935*

The Grand Illusion is Seattle's last independent and locally operated movie house. It screens off-beat/alternative films for fairly short runs and presents local filmmakers. Upstairs, you can enjoy a peaceful cup of espresso in the Grand Illusion Cafe. (See chapter 6, *Brewpubs & Coffeehouses,* for information about the Grand Illusion Cafe.) The Grand Illusion is a nonprofit organization. For membership information call (206) 329-2629.

# Guild 45th Theaters

*2115 N 45th*
*Wallingford*
*(206) 633-3353*

The Guild 45th features intellectual films. Both of the two theaters are old and comfortable in a funky sort of way. Located across the street from the Jitterbug Diner, next to My Brothers Pizza, and a few doors from Goldie's Tavern, the location makes it easy to eat and take in a movie without getting in the car. On the corner of 45th and Meridian there is a great "pub and grub" bar called Murphy's, which often features live music on weekend nights.

# Harvard Exit Theater

*807 E Roy*
*Capitol Hill*
*(206) 323-8986*

It's worth arriving early for the show just to spend time in the huge foyer of the Harvard Exit. Built and occupied by a suffragist group known as The Women's Century Club, this building reeks of times long gone. Besides the "living room" with its ancient rug, creaky floor, chess tables, sofas and fireplace (and resident ghost), there are two large theaters. The Harvard Exit screens currently popular, intellectual and foreign films. Admission to the first show is economy-priced. The Harvard Espresso is across the street and, of course, there are dozens of after-movie options nearby on Broadway.

# Kirkland Parkplace Cineplex

*3505 128th SE*
*Downtown Kirkland: Park Place Center*
*(425) 827-9000*

The Park Place Cineplex features current and popular movies. It is located right below T.G.I. Fridays, so you can make it dinner and a movie without moving your car. There are a total of six movie theaters from which to choose. While you wait, you can walk around the mall, or sit by the fountain and talk. You can also have an espresso at Starbucks or a bagel from Noah's. All shows before 6:00 P.M. are economy-priced.

## Metro Cinemas

*4500 9th*
*In the Metro Center*
*University District*
*(206) 633-0055*

The Metro Cinema has 10 theaters and screens both popular and intellectual films, The theaters are very modern and comfortable. Stella's is located on the first floor This Italian restaurant is open 24 hours a day, which is very convenient if you want to talk all night. The first show each day is economy-priced.

## Neptune Theater

*1303 NE 45th*
*University District*
*(206) 633-5545*

The Neptune Theater is located right near the "Ave" in the University District, so your choice of nearby pubs, tavs and restaurants is numerous. You can also always find a late-night coffee shop to enjoy a late-night dessert or espresso. This funky old theater features intellectual and artsy films. Across the street from the theater there is a bank with a Readyteller. The first show is economy-priced. There are also late shows on Friday nights.

## Seven Gables Theater

*911 NE 50th*
*University District*
*(206) 632-8820*

Built in what looks like an old house, the Seven Gables Theater features intellectual films. There is only one theater, and it is small and comfortably worn. The first show is economy-priced. The Seven Gables is close enough to the University District that you can eat first and be at the theater within minutes. The popular Italian restaurant Mamma Molina's is just a few doors down on Roosevelt Way.

## Uptown Cinemas

*511 Queen Anne Avenue N*
*Lower Queen Anne/Seattle*
*(206) 285-1022*

The Uptown has three theaters which screen popular movies. The complex is fairly modern. The theater is next to Kidd Valley and across from Dick's hamburgers. Lower Queen Anne has a full range of dining and drinking options within walking distance (Ristorante Pony, Queen Anne Bar and Grill, Chicago's, , Duke's, Vince's, Pizzeria Pagliacci, for a short list). The Seattle Center is nearby as well. First show is economy-priced.

## Varsity Theater

*4329 University Way NE*
*University District*
*(206) 632-3131*

The Varsity features mostly intellectual films, but you can also catch the popular shows. There are three theaters, so you can usually find something you'll like. Located right on the University of Washington "Ave," you will see all sorts of interesting people inside and outside of the theater. Restaurants, bars and coffee shops are plentiful along the Ave, and in the general vicinity. All shows before 6:00 P.M. are economy-priced.

# Chapter 8

# Dancing, Music & Club-Hopping

*W*elcome to Seattle night life! The Pacific Northwest is a haven of night spots offering every type of music imaginable. Famous for its 'grunge' rock, Seattle has turned out some of the biggest chart-breaking bands of all time. The 'Emerald City' proudly hosts some of the best live jazz clubs west of New Orleans, and has launched more than a few comedians from the nationally acclaimed comedy Improv. The following selections are Seattle favorites and will definitely provide a glimpse into what's happening late night around Puget Sound.

## The Ballard Firehouse

*Live Music/Full Bar/Food*
*3429 Russell Avenue NW*
*Ballard*
*(206) 784-3516*

This Seattle landmark is a must. The legendary former brick fire station offers live music seven nights a week. The venue includes local talent as well as major recording artists. Seattle's diversity is well-represented by offering all types of music from jazz to heavy metal. The cover charge varies with the band. Tickets are available at the door or through Ticketmaster at (206) 628-0888.

The Firehouse serves Italian cuisine, including "Louie's famous pizza," with a price range from $6.00-$10.00. Lunch is served Monday–Friday from 11:30 A.M. to 3:00 P.M. Dinner is offered seven days a week from 6:00 P.M. to closing. The live music starts at 9:30 P.M. daily and plays until closing. The Ballard Firehouse offers a full bar and accepts major credit cards and cash only. You must be twenty-one to enter and identification is required.

## Charlie's Little Pebble Bar

*Full Bar/Food/Darts & Pull-tabs*
*7001 Seaview Avenue NW*
*Ballard*
*(206) 783-8338*

The Little Pebble Bar is a charming waterfront establishment frequented by locals and fishermen from all over the world. With its quiet, relaxed atmosphere and reasonable drink prices, it's a great place to talk over cocktails while enjoying the view of Shilshole Bay in Puget Sound. Outdoor seating is available in the restaurant and in the bar.

We found both the staff and patrons at Charlie's to be very friendly. Conveniently located between the Ballard Locks and Shilshole Bay Marina, Charlie's features Happy Hour from 4:00-7:00 P.M. daily, with specials on appetizers and drinks—an enjoyable addition to a day spent in historic Ballard. Breakfast is served daily from 7:00 A.M. to 11:00 A.M., lunch from 11:00 A.M. to 3:00 P.M., and dinners from 5:00 P.M. to 9:00 P.M. You must be twenty-one to enter the bar and identification is required. Charlie's accepts major credit cards and cash only.

# Giggles Comedy Nite Club

*Full Bar/Food/Stand-Up Comedy*
*53rd and Roosevelt*
*Roosevelt District/Seattle*
*(206) 526-5653 or (206) 526-JOKE*

Giggles is the only comedy club in the Seattle area to present national touring headliners. You'll see them on stage on Sundays. Excellent up-and-coming local comedy acts appear on other days. You might be able to say you saw a future Seinfeld or Roseanne right here. As you'd expect, dress is casual—all the better to kick back and enjoy the laughs. The crowd is usually in the twenty to fifty age range. The club offers a full menu and full bar.

Thursday through Sunday shows start at 8:00 P.M.; Saturday there's also one at 10:00 P.M. For all shows, arrive at least a half-hour ahead of time. You can be any age to see the 8:00 shows, but you must be twenty-one or over for the 10:00 show. Call ahead for reservations. Seating is first-come, first served, so arrive early for the best seats.

# Swannie's-Comedy Underground

*Full Bar/Stand-Up Comedy*
*222 S Main*
*Seattle*
*(206) 622-4550*

Stand-up comedy in a nightclub atmosphere. Monday and Tuesday are open mike comedy showcase nights and have been the launching pad for many well-known comedians. Sunday is variety night, and anything can—and does—happen during these performances. Swannie's is conveniently located directly underneath Swannie's Bar & Grille in Pioneer Square in the heart of downtown Seattle. A full bar and appetizers are offered. The laughter starts at 8:30 P.M. nightly.

Those with sensitive ears, take heed, as the management is not responsible for portions of the language used by the performers.

The crowd is all ages and dress is casual. The Comedy Underground is a twenty-one and over club. Identification is required. Swannie's accepts major credit cards and cash only. The schedule is constantly changing, so call the club for current information.

## Conor-Byrne's Public House

*Traditional Irish Pub/Live Music*
*5140 Ballard Avenue NW*
*Ballard/Seattle*
*(206) 784-3640*

This is a friendly, traditional Irish pub which features set dancing every Tuesday at 8:30 P.M., and live bands every Friday and Saturday night. Sunday at 9 P.M., join in the Irish seisiun [music jam session]. This casual place has great appetizers for a modest price and a lively twenty-one to seventy-year-old crowd. This is definitely Seattle's home of Irish music. Conor Byrne's accepts major credit cards and cash only. Call for updated band information and theme nights.

## The Crocodile

*Full Bar/Food/Live Music*
*2200 Second Avenue*
*Seattle*
*(206) 441-5611*

This is one of Seattle's most famous rock clubs. In its sixth successful year, the 'Croc' has gained national fame with its steady presentations of local and national rock bands. Open seven nights a week, with varying showtimes, it is highly recommended that you arrive early as it is generally a full house. This is definitive modern rock geared at the twenty to thirty-five-year-old crowd. The food is good and the service is friendly, but the crowd is what makes this nightspot so interesting. Ticket prices range from $7.00-$20.00. Call the Crocodile for an updated schedule. This is a twenty-one and over club, and identification is required at the door. Major credit cards and cash accepted.

# The Downunder

*Full Bar/Dancing*
*2407 First Street*
*Seattle*
*(206) 728-4053*

A lively addition to the Seattle club scene, the Downunder has dancing Wednesday through Saturday nights beginning at 10:00 P.M. On Wednesdays, there is no cover and the D.J. spins tunes from the '80s. Thursday is 'brew' tasting night, with one dollar samples of dozens of microbrews. Friday and Saturday nights are hoppin' until four A.M. with a wide variety of music aimed at the twenty-one to forty crowd. There is a $5.00 cover, with various drink specials during Happy Hour from 10-11 P.M. Parking can be a challenge if arriving after 11 P.M. Dress is casual.

Due to its popularity, call the Downunder for updates regarding special promotions and theme nights.

# GameWorks

*Games/Microbrewery/Food/Music Videos*
*1511 Seventh Avenue*
*Seattle*
*(206) 521-0952*

For the very young at heart, GameWorks offers interactive video games which should require seat belts. Offering more than 250 games at $.25 to $4.00 each, there is something for everyone's budget. The nightclub is upstairs overlooking the main gaming room. Large monitors play the latest music videos at a volume that allows for conversation. Conveniently located next to Planet Hollywood in downtown Seattle, we recommend a stop at GameWorks for a local microbrew and a game or two. The crowd is diverse in age and dress; pretty much anything goes here. There is no cover to enter GameWorks, however between 8 and 10 P.M. anyone under eighteen must be accompanied by an adult. After 10 P.M. GameWorks is open to eighteen years and older only. The nightclub is open to ages twenty-one and over; identification is required. GameWorks accepts major credit cards and cash only.

## Dimitriou's Jazz Alley

*Full Bar/Food/Live Music*
*2037 Sixth Avenue*
*(corner of Sixth and Lenora)*
*Seattle*
*(206) 441-9729*

This Seattle favorite features live jazz Tuesday through Sunday, with Monday night reserved for local artists with a following. Tuesday through Thursday and Sunday nights, the sets begin at 8:00 and 9:30 P.M. with the doors opening at 6:00 P.M. If you are not having dinner, the show is $14.50 for the first set and $11.50 for the second. Dinner guests receive a discount and preferential seating. Friday and Saturday nights, the sets begin at 8:30 and 10:30 P.M., with doors opening at 6:00 P.M. The charge for the show is $15.50 for the first set, and $12.50 for the second. Dinner patrons receive the discount as well. Jazz Alley offers an Italian Mediterranean cuisine and a full bar. The seating is on a first come, first served basis. All ages are admitted with the exception of the second sets on Friday and Saturday nights. Those shows are twenty-one and over with identification required. Tickets are available in person or through Ticketmaster at (206) 628-0888. The dress is casual to formal. The entrance to Jazz Alley is on the backside of the building. Free parking is available directly across from the entrance. Reservations for dinner or cocktails is recommended.

## Patrick's 1911 Tavern

*Irish Pub/Pool/Pull Tabs/TV*
*1911 Fourth Avenue*
*Seattle*
*(206) 345-9461*

This traditional Irish pub has been around in Seattle since 1923. It's open seven days a week, 10:00 A.M. until 2:00 A.M. Serving microbrews, beer, wine as well as nonalcoholic beverages, Patrick's has bar snacks available for a reasonable charge. There are pool tables and, if you're the competitive type, you might want to participate in one of the tournaments held every Sunday at 7:00

151

P.M. Patrick's features 40 different pull tab games and sports TV. Located in the heart of downtown Seattle, this pub has a diverse clientele, ranging from twenty-one to sixty. Accepts major credit cards and cash only.

## Pier 70—Iguana Cantina

*Full Bar/Food/Dancing*
*2815 Alaskan Way*
*Seattle*
*(206) 728-7071*

This longtime Seattle nightspot has continued to provide a lively, hip atmosphere to the twenty-one to forty-five-year-old crowd. The Iguana Cantina is open Wednesday through Sunday nights, with Happy Hour each night from 4:00-7:00 P.M. Wednesday night is 'ladies' night,' where it is not uncommon to see Seattle's pro athletes jammin' to Top 40 tunes. Thursday is Disco night with rotating weekly drink specials. Friday night houses the longest-running R & B show in Seattle, hosted by KUBE Radio, 93.3 FM, and DJ Eric Powers. Saturday spins Top 40 dance music, and Sunday features the Northwest Comedy and Jazz Showcase. You must be over twenty-one to get in Iguana Cantina, and identification is required. Dress is casual to formal. Although it's in a convenient waterfront location, parking can be a challenge. Call for updated theme nights and promotions.

## Pioneer Square

*First Avenue-Downtown Seattle*
*North of the Kingdome*

Pioneer Square is located in the old town section of the city. All avenues of music and food are offered. The atmosphere is casual and extremely lively. Not the place to go for a quiet talk and a drink. The typical age range is from twenty-one to forty, and a good time is virtually guaranteed. On Friday and Saturday nights, Pioneer Square offers one joint cover charge for admittance into eight different bars. The bars accept major credit cards and cash only. The following are a few of the bars included in the joint cover:

### The Bohemian

*111 Yesler Way*
*(206) 447-1514*

### Doc Maynard's

*610 First Avenue*
*(206) 628-4649*

### The Central Saloon

*207 First Avenue*
*(206) 622-0209*

### J & M Cafe

*201 First Avenue*
*(206) 292-0663*

### Old Timers Cafe

*620 First Avenue*
*(206) 623-9800*

### Larry's Greenfront Cafe

*209 First Avenue*
*(206) 624-7665*

### New Orleans Restaurant

*114 First Avenue*
*(206) 622-2563*

### Merchants Cafe

*109 Yesler Way*
*(206) 624-1515*

## The Riverside Inn

*Full Bar/Food/Dancing*
*14060 Interurban S*
*Tukwila*
*(206) 244-5400*

A longtime Seattle establishment, the Riverside Inn is clearly the place to go for good ole' Country Western food and dancing. The restaurant serves down-home cookin' seven nights a week for a moderate price. The bar opens at 10 P.M. nightly. This is a great place to meet people and learn the latest line dances. Don't forget your hat and boots; this is the real thing!

The Riverside accepts major credit cards and cash only. The clientele spans the generations—roughly age twenty-one to eighty—and a good time is definitely in store for everyone. Call for the seasonal hours and special promotions.

# The Romper Room

*Full Bar/Food/ Dancing*
*106 First Avenue N*
*Seattle*
*(206) 284-5003*

This downtown nightspot is a must. The Romper Room is a showcase of public art displays by numerous local artists. This eclectic club also serves as a career launch pad for many of Seattle's future DJs. The Romper Room offers a moderately priced restaurant and full bar with plenty of conversation pieces to marvel at. The staff is friendly and the owner, Keith Robbins, is not only charming, but entertaining and intelligent as well. His groundbreaking art displays have inspired many Seattle tavern's decor. Thursday through Saturday, the Romper Room spins music from the '70s, '80s and '90s. The cover charge varies throughout the week. This club is twenty-one and over, and identification is required. Major credit cards and cash only accepted.

# Tropix Cafe/Beach Club

*Full Bar/Food/Games/Sports/Dancing*
*332 Fifth Avenue N*
*Seattle*
*(206) 441-2700*

Look out Frankie and Annette! Tropix Cafe and Beach Club could make you forget that you're in downtown Seattle. No rain in here! The food and drinks are competently served by a young staff in a wide range of beach attire. This is a hoppin' place geared for the college crowd, but attracting ages twenty-one to forty-five. Wednesday continues to be a successful 'Ladies Night,' with no cover for ladies and dollar cocktails all night. Thursday is 'college night': bring in a current college i.d., and drink fifty-cent drafts all night. Friday and Saturday nights are consistently busy with Seattle DJ's spinning Top 40 dance music. A great place to watch people of all ages. The dress leans toward the trendy side. Tropix is a twenty-one and over club, and proper identification is required. The Beach Club does accept major credit cards and cash only. Call for updated theme nights and special promotions.

Stepping Out in Seattle

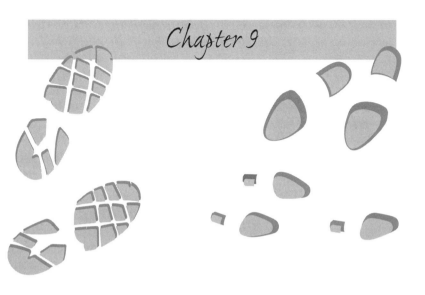

# Parks, Picnics & Walks

$G$ reater Seattle is full of terrific places to take a walk, explore a park, pack a picnic, or just enjoy a beautiful view. You can enjoy these by yourself, or with friends or a date. And many of these areas allow that special four-legged friend! So, dig out your tennis shoes, grab a friend and go!

# PARKS

Visiting a park can be romantic or fun, depending on your mood and who you're with. You can fly a kite at Gas Works Park, or have a picnic for two in the Arboretum. All you need is a sense of adventure, someone you like, and a park in mind. Please be careful when choosing a park; late-night dates in dark parks aren't safe. I recommend a sunset picnic—safe and beautiful. Don't rule out park outings, just use your common sense.

## Eastside Parks

The Eastside has plenty of parks to choose from. Here are a few of my favorites:

**Bellevue Botanical Garden** (12001 Main Street) offers 36 acres of display gardens, rolling hills, woodlands, meadows and wetlands. The Yao Garden is a secluded spot for a romantic stroll. The park has a picnic area with tables, plenty of parking and trails for exploring. The Lake-to Lake Trail, which runs from Lake Sammamish to Lake Washington, runs through the park grounds. Dogs are allowed on the Lake-to Lake Trail, but no dogs are allowed inside the Bellevue Botanical Garden. The park is open daily from 7:30 A.M. to dusk and the Visitor Center is open from 10:00 A.M. to 4:00 P.M.

**Bellevue Downtown Park** is tucked away in Downtown Bellevue, across from Bellevue Square at 4th and 100th. The park has a trail (great for walking or jogging), benches, rushing fountains, and beautiful landscaping. If you plan it right, you can enjoy the beauty of the sunset against the mirrored buildings.

**Kirkland Waterfront Parks** run along Lake Washington Boulevard and make a great walk or perfect picnic place. Moving from South to North along Lake Washington Boulevard, the first park is Houghton Beach Park, right across from Kidd Valley (burgers make great picnics). Houghton has benches, grass, a dock, swimming and a view of Seattle beyond the lake. Next is Marsh Park, which also has benches and access to the water. Third is David E. Brink Park, also with benches and water access. Finally, you'll find the Kirkland Marina and Park. The marina has benches, statues, a fountain and great view of Lake Washington and Seattle. If you're up for adventure, check out an Argosy Lake Cruise or parasailing at the marina. Park your car down in the marina parking lot and walk to Houghton Beach and back. It's a beautiful walk along a paved sidewalk.

**Luther Burbank Park** is on Mercer Island (84th Avenue SE), and runs along picturesque Lake Washington, with views of the lake, Bellevue and Seattle. Luther Burbank has picnic benches, grassy fields, paved paths, a boat dock, swimming, tennis courts, a fishing dock, and a children's play area. The park has an off-leash area where dogs can run free. In other parts of the park they must be on a leash. In either place you must clean up after them.

**Marymoor Park** in Redmond is gorgeous. One of its highlights is the adjacent paved Sammamish River Trail, which stretches out for miles. You can park your car at Marymoor and then bike, walk, run or roller-blade for hours. Stop off at one of the wineries or breweries in Woodinville. (See chapter 4, *Coffeehouses, Brewpubs, and Wine Tours*, for more information). Marymoor also has picnic benches, sporting events, a museum and a children's play area. One of the special features of this park is the dog run. This special spot is where your dog (and many others) can run free and play in the nearby stream. It's great fun watching these dogs frolic in the water together. This is the perfect place to take a friend (either four-legged and two-legged!)

**Medina Beach** at the end of Evergreen Point Road has a beautiful view of Lake Washington, the Seattle skyline and Mercer Island. It sits right in front of the Medina Police Department, so safety isn't an issue. During the summer expect a lot of kids, but during the off-season, the beach is peaceful and beautiful. The park was the original ferry boat landing to Seattle, and has picnic tables and swimming.

## Seattle Parks

Seattle has many beautiful parks and you can get a complete guide to Seattle parks from the Seattle Department of Parks and Recreation, by calling (206) 684-4075. The parks below are "special places" for you to explore.

**Alki Beach** runs along Alki Avenue SW and has the feel of a vacation beach town. Only this beach has one of the finest views of the Seattle skyline imaginable. The walk is paved and perfect for a romantic sunset stroll, or get an order of fish and chips from Spuds and have a picnic on the beach. There are also grassy areas along the path and benches to sit and admire the view from. (For more information on Alki, see *Noteworthy Neighborhoods* in chapter 4).

**Capitol Hill Park and View** (on 15th between E Garfield and E Olin Streets) is kitty-corner from the Lake View Cemetery. The park provides benches, grass, interesting sculptures and a spectacular view of Lake Washington, the Eastside and Mount Baker. One special spot in the park is a bench built around a tree, which sits out on the point, with the view almost on top of you. Take a picnic, read poetry, or just sit and talk. The pure beauty of this view is both relaxing and exhilarating.

**Discovery Park** in Magnolia (36th West and West Government Way), is a huge park stretching from woods to water. In addition to trails, beach, a lighthouse, picnic tables, children's play area, wide-open fields, and woodlands, the park houses Daybreak Star Arts and Indian Cultural Center. (The center is open from 10:00 A.M. to 5:00 P.M. Monday-Friday and from 12:00 noon-5:00 P.M. Sunday). One of the best picnic spots in the park is located directly across from the Daybreak Center. These picnic tables look out over Puget Sound to the north with views of Edmonds and Mount Baker. I highly recommend this spot!

**Freeway Park** (Sixth and Seneca in Downtown Seattle) is unique because it stretches across the freeway (hence the name). Although, I don't recommend hanging around the park at night, this is a wonderful place for a lunch date, especially if you work downtown. If you don't work in the city, check out the park on a weekend. There are paved paths and benches, as well as the hum of the freeway below!

**Gas Works Park** (N Northlake Way and Meridian N) is one of Seattle's originals. There is ample parking, rolling green hills, walks, picnic tables and, of course, the iron gas work machinery. The child in you will love exploring the old machines, and when weather permits, this is the perfect place to fly a kite! The park looks out over Lake Union toward the city. It's a great place to watch the sunset while enjoying a pizza from the Northlake Tavern or fish and chips from Ivar's (see chapter 2, *Restaurants*, for information on both).

**Green Lake** offers a little bit of everything for the outdoor-loving pair. Green Lake Park runs around the lake, along East Green Lake Drive N and West Green Lake Drive N. The park has a paved path for bikes, joggers, roller-bladers and walkers. You can also enjoy water sports such as paddleboating, windsurfing and swimming. The park has benches and a few picnic tables, or bring a blanket and take advantage of the lake view from one of the grassy areas. (For information on rentals at Green Lake, see Gregg's, listed in chapter 5, *Indoor & Outdoor Play*).

**Madison Park** is another park with a gorgeous view of Lake Washington. Madison Park is at the end of East Madison on 43rd. The park is small and can be very crowded on summer afternoons. There is a beach for swimming, a children's play area and some grass. The real draw of the park is the view and the Madison Park shopping and eateries nearby. The park makes a great stroll after dining at any of the wonderful restaurants Madison Park has to offer. (For more information on Madison Park, see the *Noteworthy Neighborhoods* section in chapter 4.)

**Myrtle Edwards** (Alaskan Way between West Bay and West Thomas) runs along Puget Sound and has views to the west and north of the Sound, Alki Point, and the San Juan Islands. This is a spectacular spot, especially for newcomers and visitors to Seattle. The park offers public fishing, a separate bike and walking trail (1.25 miles), and a few picnic tables. If you're set on a picnic, you might want to bring a blanket along to sit on. Dogs are allowed at Myrtle Edwards, but they must be on a leash.

**Parsons Garden** is tucked away among the houses on West Highland Drive at Seventh West. The garden is host to weddings during the summer months and is a truly romantic spot. The secluded, private garden has a short trail that runs around the garden. It is the ideal spot for a romantic picnic for two. There are no tables, but eating on a blanket under a tree is much more romantic anyway! Across the street, enjoy a breathtaking view of Puget Sound and the city skyline.

**The Queen Anne View** is just a few blocks from Parsons Garden on West Highland Drive at Third. This park has a view of Seattle to take your breath away. On a clear day, you can see Mount Rainier behind the city skyline. It also looks out over Puget Sound towards Alki Point. There are benches, but no tables. Stairs lead down to a lower section of the park with a children's play area. However, the main attraction is the view. Be sure to bring your camera on this trip!

**Piers 62 & 63** are home to the Waterfront Park next to the Seattle Aquarium. This park is built on piers over Puget Sound, with benches, fountain and a great view of the Sound. The park is conveniently located near many food and shopping establishments. On a warm summer, I suggest an ice cream cone and a walk along the pier.

**Volunteer Park** (15th E and E Prospect) is high atop Capitol Hill. The park is home to the conservatory, which was built in 1912, and maintains five distinct simulated climates. The jungle and desert exhibits are very interesting. (There is no admission fee to the conservatory and the phone number is (206) 684-4743. The Seattle Asian Art Museum is also located in Volunteer Park (for more information on the Seattle Asian Museum, see chapter 1, *Cultural Attractions*). Volunteer Park has trails, grassy meadows and makes a great destination.

# PICNICS

A picnic's casual pace allows you to focus on the place and the food and each other. It allows you the quiet time to explore mutual interests. If it's your first picnic, it can become a memory both of you will always associate with the birth of your relationship. If it's your 100th and counting, you can activate all those memories. Your only task is to be ready to take advantage of the area's festive foods and perfect picnic spots—food and places made for romance and memories.

Filling a basket with Seattle's choice foods will not be a problem because you'll each have your own picnic favorites to contribute. It's choosing the perfect spot for your outing that will take a little more thought. This is not a choice to be made lightly. The place has to possess significance without being overwhelming. To make it easier, choose from among the following 10 couple-tested picnic destinations. The list is a mixture of city gardens, quiet water-views, and lofty vistas, each chosen to inspire a particular theme for your picnic and to be experienced in whichever season love blossoms or seeks renewal.

## The Rose Garden at Woodland Park Zoo

*5500 Phinney Avenue N*
*Seattle*
*(206) 684-4800*

Just to the south of the zoo and behind high walls and wrought-iron gates, you'll step into Guy Phinney's 1890s tea garden—a quiet, intensely fragrant rose bower. One hundred and ninety species representing every rose hue imaginable are planted in ornate, manicured Victorian splendor. If you can talk your companion into donning vintage clothing, so much the better.

Because there are no tables here, choose picnic foods that are easy to eat with your fingers or from your lap. Benches are scattered among the sculptured shrubbery and reflecting ponds and you can picnic on one of them, or spread a picnic rug if you prefer the plush lawn. The heady fragrance will reach you wherever you sit.

Then, after your picnic, gather the wind-blown petals at your feet to make potpourri or pressed rose beads.

Directions: From I-5 take the NE 50th Street exit and drive west. The south entrance of the zoo is located at N 50th and Fremont Avenue N.

## Chateau Ste. Michelle Winery

*14111 NE 145th Street*
*Woodinville*
*(425) 488-1133*

You'll have no trouble creating a French theme for this romantic picnic destination. Approach from either side via foot or bike and the Burke-Gilman Trail (which traces the Sammamish River to the east and Lake Washington to the west). Bring bread, Brie, and fruit in your basket or, if you wish to appear spontaneous, purchase pâté and a bottle of wine at the gift shop. Everything you need for a picnic is available there.

Choose a shaded spot on the lawn, then lean back and imagine that the chateau and its grounds are yours. You might even wish to include pad and pastels to create a truly French Impressionist memory of your outing among the vineyards.

Mature trees and flower beds border wandering paths, fountains, ponds, and grassy spots, creating outdoor "rooms," the largest of which is the outdoor amphitheater. In summer, Shakespeare and jazz play to romance and picnickers under the stars (see page 00 for additional details).

Directions: From I-405, take Exit 23A (SR 522, Monroe-Wenatchee) to the Woodinville exit. Turn south (right) off the exit and continue three blocks to NE 175th Street. Turn west (right) and follow the road to the stop sign. Turn south (left) on Highway 202 and drive approximately two miles to the winery entrance.

## NOAA Grounds

*7600 Sand Point Way NE*
*Seattle*
*(206) 526-6385*

For an unobstructed, unpopulated, and inspirational water view of Lake Washington, bike or stroll along the Burke-Gilman Trail to NE 70th Street, and down to NOAA (National Oceanic and Atmospheric Administration) property and its collection of outdoor art. Cinder paths cut across wetland grasses and sanctuaries for waterfowl, and through and among sculpted berms and piers and a sound garden built to capture and play windsongs. It's a wondrous place, perfect for the quiet exploration of your relationship.

Except for quick-stop stores on Sand Point Way, there are few places to obtain picnic ingredients nearby, so plan to pack your picnic before starting out.

Directions: From I-5, take the NE 65th Street exit. Drive east on NE 65th Street to Sand Point Way NE. Turn north. Enter the NOAA gate and park near lot 1.

## Foster Island

*2700 24th Avenue East*
*Museum of History & Industry*
*Trail begins in parking lot*

Lily pads, slanted sunlight, graceful willows, and journey by canoe lend an Impressionistic air to this urban island across the ship canal from the University of Washington stadium. Pull your canoe up onto the bank and unload your feast. Whether you spread a blanket on the grass or find one of the two benches unoccupied, as they often are, you will enjoy a prime view of passing yachts and sailboats through the Montlake Cut. (See chapter 5, *Indoor & Outdoor Play* , for information on canoe rentals.)

After you've finished eating, you can stroll along the Waterfront Trail to one of the private view spots. You never know just what or whom you'll encounter as you head across the boardwalk, so be prepared for adventure. One day it might be a beret-topped juggler, the next day a pair of nude sunbathers on a hidden side platform. It's that kind of unforgettable place.

Directions: Located just north of Highway 520 and the Washington Park Arboretum. The Museum of History and Industry is located two blocks east of Montlake Boulevard. The trail begins in the northeast corner of the parking lot.

## Meridian Park

*Meridian Avenue N and N 50th Street*
*(206) 584-4081*

West of the University of Washington, in the heart of Wallingford, is a grand old building complete with weathered gazebo, estate-sized lawn, gnarled orchard, and funky gardens. These and the arched entrance on 50th and Meridian foster a Secret Garden-sort of atmosphere which surrounds the former Good Shepherd Home.

Besides the vast expanse of lawn and its orchards, you'll be able to explore and learn from the labeled and scarecrow-guarded Tilth and P-Patch gardens. Chances are, even on a sun-drenched day, you will have the park to yourself. But if you time your picnic to correspond with the annual sales and fairs held by Tilth and others on the grounds, you'll be able to purchase edible plants and take advantage of the bountiful harvests. However, you'll no longer be alone. You choose.

Directions: From I-5, take the NE 50th Street exit and drive west. Turn south (left) on Meridian Avenue North and park on the street.

## Radar Park

*SE Cougar Mountain Drive*
*Bellevue*
*(206) 296-4932*

Because very few picnickers wend their way to this small, incredible park with its million-dollar view of Lake Sammamish, it will seem as if you are the only couple in the whole wide world. In fact, because Radar Park is located high above Bellevue on Cougar Mountain, it will seem as if you're on top of the world. It's a good feeling when you're attempting to initiate a good, solid relationship or get away from the cares below.

Radar Park is worth exploring no matter what the season. Toward the end of summer, you can gather wild black raspberries and red huckleberries, and in winter, because of its high elevation, you can carve angels in the snow or attempt to identify the small animal tracks.

Directions: From I-90, take Exit 11-A. Head south on 150th Avenue SE to SE Newport Way. Turn east (left) and follow Newport Way to 164th Avenue SE. Turn south (right) and follow the road up the mountain to Cougar Mountain Way. Turn east (left) and follow the road as it curves to SE 60th Street, turn south (right) and drive one block, then right again at SE Cougar Mountain Drive. Drive approximately 3/4 mile to Radar Park's entrance gate. Park in the lot across from the lone house.

## Carl S. English, Jr., Botanical Garden

*3015 NW 54th Street*
*At Ballard Locks*
*Seattle*
*(206) 783-7059*

In days past, you could have imagined hopping aboard a flatbed by Myrtle Edwards Park and riding it as far as Golden Gardens, or hopping off just the other side of the ship canal for a picnic at the locks. In today's world, you'll have to arrive at the locks by car, foot or bike (or maybe roller blades). You can gather picnic items as you journey past the Redhook Ale Brewery pub or at one of Ballard's Scandinavian food shops.

Once you arrive, head for the terraced banks overlooking the continual parade of water traffic motoring through the locks. But don't assume that the gardens only encompass the area bordering the walk or overlooking the canal. Walk to the west and you'll soon come upon your own unclaimed spot. There you can dream of hopping trains bound for the Far North or barges to China, or. . .

Directions: From I-5, take the North 85th Street exit. Follow 85th Street west approximately three miles to 32nd Avenue NW. Turn south and drive 1½ miles to NW 54th Street and the entrance to the locks.

## The Washington State Ferries

*Colman Dock, Pier 52*
*Seattle*
*(206) 464-6400*

Embark on a dreamy adventure I call, "In the Night Ferry" (with all due apologies to Maurice Sendak's popular children's book, *In the Night Kitchen).* Start by consulting the newspaper for the posted sunset times, then park your car under the Alaskan Way Viaduct and walk onto the Bremerton ferry at the Colman Dock.

Crossing the Sound to Bremerton is one of the longest of the Washington State ferry runs, giving you ample time to open your basket, spread and enjoy its contents, and still stand at the outside rail to catch the crepuscular rays shooting from the setting sun.

On the return crossing to Seattle, you'll be able to witness the gradual lighting of the Seattle night skyline, the end to a perfect picnic.

Directions: Located at Pier 52 on Alaskan Way. From I-5, follow the signs to the "Ferry Terminal."

## Kubota Gardens

*Corner of Renton Avenue South and 51st Avenue South*
*Seattle*
*(206) 684-4081*

A tranquil, Zen-like quality envelops you as you walk down the path into Kubota Gardens, one of Seattle's newest city parks. At the foot of the hill, stones cross the first pond to a miniature island and its stone lantern. A path on the other side leads over a mound and through the trees to a view of a second pool where a crimson bridge and, in summer, yellow irises cast their rippled reflections. On the other side of the bridge, there's a winding path to the highest point of the park. On the way to the top, you'll encounter boulders carved with Japanese characters. Perhaps they and the imperial water view will inspire you to compose your own Haiku for the occasion.

Flat stones, carved benches, and grassy knolls provide several serene spots for you to celebrate the changing seasons and to share bentos (boxed picnic lunches, Japanese style).

Directions: From I-5, take the Swift Avenue/Albro Place exit. Head south and east on Swift Avenue South (it becomes South Myrtle Street) to Martin Luther King, Jr. Way South. Turn south (right) and drive one block to Renton Avenue South. Turn east (left)) and drive one block past 51st Avenue South to Lindsay Place. Turn south (right) to the park.

## Gene F. Coulon Park

*1201 Lake Washington Boulevard N*
*Renton*
*(425) 235-2560*

What if you're looking for romance during a season of cold, damp, and shortened days? What then? Do you have to abandon all thoughts of private picnics in the park? Not at all. Instead, head for one of the area's best-kept secrets and create a true Northwest tradition—an Eddie Bauer-REI style, winter picnic.

This best-kept secret is to be found on the southeast corner of Lake Washington in Renton. There, in Gene F. Coulon Park, you will find a large covered pavilion with a central firepit, perfect for cozy, toasty picnics in the middle of December.

What could be more romantic or relaxing than the glow of embers reflected in your smiles and eyes, than the licking of melted marshmallows from your chilled fingers, than the lapping of the waves and the dripping of the rain from the roof? Trust me: a winter picnic in the Northwest becomes one the two of you will never forget.

Directions: From I-405, take the NE Park Avenue and Sunset Boulevard NE exit and head west toward the lake. Follow the signs to Coulon Memorial Park and turn north (right) on Lake Washington Boulevard North.

# WALKS

The popularity of walking in the Seattle area is hardly surprising. The area tends to attract folks of outdoorsy bent; its incredible collage of mountains, forest, islands, saltwater, lakes, streams, and cityscape provides an unsurpassed backdrop for pedestrian pursuits; and its excellent network of parks and trails offer walks for every age and taste.

For first dates, a walk, either by itself or combined with a meal or movie or whatever, can't be beat. For starters, walking is by nature more casual than other types of dates. It's a date where both parties can pretend they aren't really dating. You know, we're just walking. Nothing really on the line. Just an opportunity to get acquainted in a nonstressful setting.

Second—let's face it—walking is cheap, and isn't it nice to know that two people can get together to do something fun, without spending a fortune? Third, walking suggests that you are vastly more complex and sensitive than all those other potential partners your companion could be spending time with. Finally, walking is a good way to burn off nervous first-date energy, a soothing alternative to fidgeting or rattling on about your roommate or whatever.

For friends and long-time couples, walking remains a rewarding, no-hassle, low-budget, energizing way to connect. When you're walking, you can talk or be silent, as your mood dictates. No one expects you to entertain while you're walking.

Date walks, of course, must be romantic, depending on your definition of romance. If that definition includes slogging, sweaty browed and burdened like a mule, up the side of a mountain (and why not?), we recommend turning to one of the several excellent hiking guides to this region. But if romance for you means sunsets, city lights, salt air, and mountain views, all with clean shoes and no blisters and a pace suitable for hand-holding, then the walks described in this section are for you. The walks described below are either in or near Seattle, and those that are out of town are close to outlying restaurants and other attractions for the romantically inclined. All are easy, more or less level, jaunts that are suitable for people of all ages. Those which are wheel-chair accessible are noted below. Hand-holding, of course, is optional.

# Distance and Pace

The distances given for each walk are one way, unless noted otherwise. Double the figures to calculate the distance of a round trip. Why, you ask, aren't round-trip distances given in the first place? Because you don't have to walk the entire length of a route. You can turn around a third of the way, a half of the way, or whatever. So, the total, round-trip distance will be different for each couple. Providing the one-way figure makes calculating that total easier.

If time is a factor, use the following table to estimate how much time you'll need:

| Pace | Distance Covered in One Hour |
| --- | --- |
| *Leisurely* | *1.5 to 2 miles* |
| *Normal* | *2.5 to 3 miles* |
| *Brisk* | *3.5 to 4 miles* |
| *Fast* | *Please, not on a date!* |
| | *You're missing the point.* |

# A Note on Shoes

Most of the walks described below are suitable for street shoes. On a couple of the walks, you should really wear athletic shoes to spare both your feet and your dress shoes. The shoe rating for each walk is noted below.

Finally, let's get real about high heels. They're engineered for showing off women's legs, not for walking. So guys, if you plan to go for an after-dinner walk, tell your date so she can choose whether to bring along her walking shoes. If she chooses not to, save the walk for another time. And women, give yourself a break. If you must wear high heels before or after your walk, at least take along a second pair of shoes for the pedestrian portion of the evening. Or suggest, tactfully of course, that it might not be the best idea to walk around Green Lake before attending *Aida*.

## Alki Beach

Join the young and restless along Seattle's only stretch of waterfront that feels like a real beach, you know, such as they have in Oregon and California. The sand, the classic beach cottages, and the pervasive smell of saltwater, sunscreen, and deep-fried cooking all combine to persuade us that we are in Florence, Bandon, Half Moon Bay, Laguna, or countless other seaside resorts between Astoria and San Diego. This is the spot for the midsummer bronze-body beach date, in which case you can walk barefooted the entire length of the beach from Duwamish Head to Alki Point. Or come here after dinner, as the sun is setting, and look west to the purpling Olympics and east, across Elliott Bay, to the towers of downtown Seattle. Or come by day and join the beautiful bodies who are sun bathing, cruising Alki Avenue, eating, hanging out, and watching one another. To reach Alki Beach, take the West Seattle Freeway to Harbor Avenue SW and drive north around Duwamish Head to the beach. Park wherever you find room. Wheelchair access. Street shoes okay.

Distance: 2 miles one way.

## Myrtle Edwards Park and Elliott Bay Park

Myrtle Edwards and Elliott Bay parks together form a narrow strip of glory extending northward along the Seattle waterfront for about a mile and a quarter from the public parking lot where Alaskan Way turns left onto Broad Street. No one pays much attention to where one park ends and its neighbor begins, but the official boundary is roughly opposite Thomas Street. The paved path passes public sculptures, benches for foot resting and view gazing, fitness stations, and a fishing pier en route to its northern terminus at 16th Street, near the Port of Seattle's Ellis Island for Japanese automobiles. On a clear day, face the Olympics as you head north, and Mt. Rainier and downtown Seattle as you return south. The fishing pier is a good turnaround for northbound walkers, and if you time your excursion carefully, you can watch the sun set over the Olympics from one of the several benches on the pier. The parks are close to the restaurants and other attractions of the lively Lower Queen Anne neighborhood and only slightly farther from the Pike Place Market and downtown. Except on the warmest days, figure on taking a jacket. This area is consistently more windy than almost anywhere else in town. Wheelchair accessible. Street shoes okay.

Distance: 1.5 miles one way.

## Magnolia Bluff

From Magnolia Bluff, the view westward across the Sound to the Olympics, and south to downtown Seattle and Mt. Rainier, is so outstanding that this essentially neighborhood stroll draws people from all over town, especially on summer evenings for the sunset show. The elegant houses facing Magnolia Boulevard (for that matter, throughout this affluent neighborhood) provide a visual bonus in the form of beautiful, manicured gardens, which achieve an overwhelming climax of color in April and May, when the rhododendrons and Azaleas are in bloom. Except on the warmest summer days, you are likely to need jackets for this often windy blufftop walk. To reach Magnolia Bluff, drive Elliott Avenue West and follow signs to Magnolia. Cross the Magnolia Bridge and follow W Galer to a stop sign. Turn left on Howe Street, cross a bridge, and shortly veer left on Magnolia Boulevard, which curves south, then swings west to the edge of the bluff. Park along the street or in the parking lot at the viewpoint. Walk north or south along the bluff as whim dictates. Northward, the road veers away from the edge of the bluff in about one-half mile, a good place to turn around. More ambitious or preoccupied walkers can continue past posh estates and fine homes to Discovery Park, just over a mile north of the viewpoint. Wheelchair accessible. Street shoes okay.

Distance: 1 mile one way.

## South Bluff

Seattle abounds in outstanding places to view the sun setting over the Olympics, but Discovery Park's South Bluff is the ultimate romantic, blow-the-top-of-your-head-off sunset viewpoint in town. Add a ferry or two, or sailboats tacking in the twilight, and the two of you may just swoon straight away. Since South Bluff occupies the westernmost point of land in all of Seattle, the rest of the city doesn't intrude between you and the vastness to the west. And since South Bluff is accessible only to those who are willing to walk about a half mile from the Discovery Park's South Parking Lot, your companions will be people who are as dedicated to sunsettery as you, and there will be fewer of them than at the more popular roadside viewpoints. What's more, South Meadow, which stretches back from the bluff, is so vast that you won't have much trouble finding a place to yourself. Finally, the natural surroundings, free of autos, houses, and roads, complement the view as no other locale in Seattle can. To reach South Bluff, drive 15th Avenue NW to W Emerson, just south of the Ballard Bridge. Follow W Emerson past the Fishermen's Terminal to Gilman Way. Turn right and follow signs to Discovery Park. A couple of blocks before the east entrance to the park, turn left on 34th Avenue, then turn right on W Emerson (yes, you're back on Emerson again) and drive along the south boundary of the park to the entrance to the South Parking Lot. From the parking lot, follow the Loop Trail back along the entry road and onward to South Bluff. Restrooms are located at the bluff. Come early to claim a bench at the edge of the cliff. Or follow the Loop Trail a short way beyond South Meadow to South Point, where log seats and a bench await. Walking shoes recommended.

Distance: .5 mile one way.

## Green Lake

Green Lake is Seattle's finest and best-loved all-around urban walk. The sunsets are better at Myrtle Edwards Park or Magnolia Bluff, the body exhibit is more ample and varied at Alki, the view of Sound and mountains is far better at Discovery Park. But no walk in town so perfectly blends the combination of urban pleasures and natural beauty. And no walk within a day's drive of Smith Tower offers better people-watching. Everyone walks, runs, roller-blades, or bikes around Green Lake at one time or another, including the most famous names in town—TV personalities, politicians, and sports stars. On a warm summer weekend, it seems as if half of Seattle is walking around the lake, while the other half lounges on the grass watching them go by. You can combine a walk around Green Lake with dinner at one of the many fine nearby neighborhood eateries. Or you can make the lake itself the focus of your date. Either way, you can't miss. To get to Green Lake, exit I-5 at 50th, 71st, or 80th streets. Head west and follow your road map to the lake. Parking is available along the street or in one of the three parking lots around the lake. Head for the water and follow the paved two-lane trail clockwise around the lake. Park regulations, which are printed in fading white letters on the trail, state that walkers should proceed clockwise, and skaters and bicyclists counterclockwise, around the lake. This bureaucratic attempt to make the walk safer and saner for everyone may be the most universally ignored regulation in the city. Wheelchair accessible. Street shoes okay.

Distance: 2.9 miles.

## Waterfront Trail

The Waterfront Trail makes a perfect evening walk following dinner in the University District or a visit to the Museum of History and Industry. Beginning at the northeast corner of the museum parking lot, a splendid boardwalk meanders among willows, cottonwoods, cattails, and water lilies along the southern fringe of Union Bay, on Lake Washington. Ducks and geese mosey through the marsh; swallows swoop and dive overhead; great blue herons stand motionless, knee-deep in water, waiting for hapless frogs. Gaze across Union Bay to Husky Stadium, the University boat house, and Laurelhurst. On a clear day, the Cascades form a spectacular backdrop across Lake Washington to the east. Best of all, from the dating point of view, are the secluded benches located at the end of short side-trails along the way. The trail proceeds about one-half mile to Foster Island, where you can either turn around or continue southward along a broad path into the University of Washington Arboretum. To get to the Waterfront Trail, drive State Route 520 west to the Montlake exit. At the stoplight on Montlake, continue straight ahead on E Lake Washington Boulevard for one block, turn left on Park Drive, and continue to the parking lot behind the Museum of History and Industry. From the Eastside, drive 520 to the Lake Washington Boulevard exit. Turn right at the stop sign and continue to Park Drive. Wheelchair accessible. Walking shoes recommended.

Distance: .5 mile one way.

# Azalea Way

The University of Washington Arboretum is Seattle's largest woodland garden, combining native vegetation with ornamental trees and shrubs from around the world. Numerous trails meander through the Arboretum, following woodland glades, gently ascending to overlooks, winding through forest, and visiting secluded pools and small brooks. Any one of them, either by itself or combined with other activities, makes a great date walk. The Japanese Garden with its authentic handmade tea house, makes a splendid stop along the way, especially in autumn, when the Japanese maples are brilliant scarlet, crimson, and orange. The Arboretum saves its most spectacular display of color, however, for spring, when its extensive plantings of rhododendrons and azaleas burst into bloom, beginning in early April and extending through the first week in June. In normal years, this two-month riot of color reaches its climax in early May along Azalea Way, a gentle, grassy lane beginning at the Arboretum Visitor's Center and heading south for perhaps one-half mile. The sheer exuberance, abundance, and variety of color verges on the unbelievable.

For the ultimate spring date walk, work off your Sunday brunch with a hand-in-hand stroll down Azalea Way. Prepare to swoon. To get to Azalea Way, drive State Route 520 west to the Montlake exit. At the stoplight on Montlake, continue straight ahead on E Lake Washington Boulevard and, in about one-half mile, turn left on Foster Island Road. Wind around to the intersection with Arboretum Drive. Either park here, or continue on Arboretum Drive to the Visitor Center and more parking. Azalea Way begins across Arboretum Drive from the Visitor Center. Ask for directions if you get lost. From the Eastside, exit on Lake Washington Boulevard. Turn left at the stop sign, immediately left again on Foster Island Road, and proceed as described above. Approaching the Arboretum from the south, follow Lake Washington Boulevard to Arboretum Drive and keep right to the Visitor Center. Walking shoes recommended.

Distance: .75 mile one way.

## Lake Washington Boulevard

The perfect walk for a dawn date, but also great in the early evening, when the sun's last rays turn the glass towers of downtown Bellevue, across the lake, into pillars of fire. In October and November, enjoy one of Seattle's finest displays of fall color. In April and May, marvel at the multihued displays of azaleas and rhododendrons in the manicured yards that line Lake Washington Boulevard. On a clear winter day, gaze at the white Cascade crags arrayed along the eastern horizon. In summer, stop along the way to dangle your feet in the lake. If you love the roar, the crowds, the Blue Angel acrobatics, and the rooster tails of the hydroplane races, take this walk on Seafair Weekend. If you don't, take it on any other weekend but that one! All year long, watch geese, sailboats, people, and the infinite moods and shadings of Lake Washington. Begin at Seward Park and walk north to Leschi and Madrona Park—or vice-versa. Either way works. Attractions along the way, from north to south, include Madrona Park, the shops and restaurants of Leschi, the current and former I-90 bridges (the latter notable for its absence), Stan Sayres Pits, and Seward Park. Do all or part of it as the mood strikes and as time and energy allow. From Seattle, drive northeast on Madison Street to Lake Washington Boulevard, then turn right (south) and follow the sharply winding road to Madrona Park. Or follow Boren and Rainier avenues south to Genesee Street, then turn left (east) and continue to Lake Washington Boulevard. From this intersection, you can see Seward Park across Andrews Bay. Head south on Lake Washington Boulevard to the parking lot. Street shoes okay.

Distance: 5 miles one way.

## I-90 Bridge

On a warm, clear day, walk across Lake Washington on the safe, broad pedestrian-bicycle lane perched above the traffic on the north side of the new I-90 bridge, which connects Mercer Island to Seattle. Look south to Boeing, Renton, and Mount Rainier, and north to the Evergreen Point Bridge and beyond. Unless you have a boat, this walk is the best way to experience the great size and beauty of Lake Washington. And it is required therapy for west-or east-bound commuters who barely look at the lake as they hurtle, teeth-clenched and eyes glazed, across the bridges each morning and afternoon. This route is mostly the domain of bicycles, so keep right and stay alert. Most riders coming from behind will alert you to their approach with an "On your left." One true precaution: avoid this walk during storms, when high winds and driving rain can pose a hazard, mainly in the form of hypothermia, to pedestrians. From the Seattle side, pick up the route at the junction of 35th Avenue S and S Irving. Parking is available on the street. Or you can park below the I-90 bridge on Portal Place and walk up the steps to the entrance onto the bridge. From the Mercer Island side, park in the public parking lot on W Mercer Way, immediately north of the freeway. The paved path runs along the south side of the parking lot. Wheelchair accessible. Street shoes okay.

Distance: 1 mile one way.

## Lake Hills Greenbelt

Bellevue's Lake Hills Greenbelt is a narrow corridor of fields and woods extending from Larsen Lake in the north to Phantom Lake in the south. The Greenbelt is a short way from restaurants and other attractions in the Crossroads and Overlake areas, and not much farther from downtown Bellevue. The trail is broad, well-maintained, and easy on the feet. Wildlife is plentiful; you may even spot bald eagles working their way up and down the Greenbelt from nests near Lake Sammamish. In season, you can buy blueberries from the active blueberry farm surrounding Larsen Lake, and corn from the produce stand near the parking lot at the junction of 156th Avenue SE and SE. 16th Street. From this parking lot, you can walk either south to Phantom Lake or north to Larsen Lake. Or you can park at the Larsen Lake parking area, located on 148th Avenue SE between Main Street and SE 8th Street. Walking shoes recommended.

Distance: 1 mile one way from Larsen Lake to Phantom Lake.

# Mercer Slough Nature Park

Located a couple of miles south of downtown Bellevue, the Mercer Slough Nature Park is an excellent place to walk any time of day or year. The park extends north-south on both sides of Mercer Slough, a narrow channel linking Kelsey Creek and Lake Washington. This natural park, combining, marsh, woods, blueberry fields, and meandering channels, currently contains five miles of trails, with additional miles to be completed by the end of 1992, and more yet on the drawing board. Existing trails consist mainly of boardwalks, woodchip paths, and paved walkways. By early 1993, a new bridge should cross Mercer Slough, linking the Overlake Blueberry Farm on the west with the old Bellefields Nature Park on the east. For now, the two best walks are the Bellefields loop and the boardwalk beginning at the Sweolocken Canoe Boat Launch, on Bellevue Way, just north of I-90.

From the parking lot at the boat launch, follow the boardwalk south toward Lake Washington, then turn left and walk across and above the wetlands to 118th Avenue SE. Or drive south of SE 8th Street onto 118th Avenue SE and continue one-half mile to the small parking lot on the right, near the entrance to the old Bellefields Nature Park. From this parking lot, you can either follow the path that heads southward, parallel to the road, or you can follow the loop trail that begins a few yards south of the parking lot, plunging downslope through woods into the heart of the wetland. Since the Mercer Slough Nature Park trail network is currently under development, be sure to check with the Bellevue Parks Department Ranger (425) 451-7225 or (425)-455-6881 for the latest information on which trails have been completed and are open to the public. Wheelchair accessible. Walking shoes recommended.

Distance: 0.5 to 5 miles, depending on your route.

# Calendar of Events

Seattle's diversity makes it a great place for friends, couples and singles. Why not take advantage of the area's many special activities and celebrations? This Calendar of Events is not a complete list of events in the Greater Seattle area. (That would cover an entire book itself!) Those listed make especially fun outings, and are meant to be shared with a friend. For a complete list of events, call the Seattle-King County Convention and Visitors Bureau at (206) 461-5800.

## JANUARY

### Art Grazing
*Bellevue*
*(425) 453-1223*

## FEBRUARY

### Chinese New Year
*International District/Seattle*
*(206) 223-0623*

### Fat Tuesday, Mardi Gras Celebration
*Pioneer Square/Seattle*
*(206) 622-2563*

## MARCH

### Irish Festival
*Seattle Center/Seattle*
*(206) 684-7200*

# APRIL

## Cherry Blossom Festival

*Seattle Center/Seattle*
*(206) 684-7135*

## Daffodil Festival

*Puyallup*
*(253) 627-6176*

# MAY

## Northwest Folklife Festival

*Seattle Center/Seattle*
*(206) 684-7300*

## Market Festival

*Pike Place Market/Seattle*
*(206) 624-3570*

## Seattle International Film Festival

*Seattle*
*(206) 324-9996*

# JUNE

## Out to Lunch Concerts

*Seattle*
*(206) 623-0340*

# JULY

## Bite of Seattle

*Seattle Center/Seattle*
*(206) 684-7200*

## Fourth of July-Ivar's

*Seattle Waterfront*
*(206) 587-6500*

## Heritage Festival

*Redmond*
*(425) 296-2964*

## King County Fair

*Enumclaw*
*(253) 296-8888*

## Pacific Northwest Arts & Crafts Fair

*Downtown Bellevue*
*(425) 454-4900*

## SeaFair Celebration

*(Begins at the end of July and runs through August)*
*Various sites throughout the Seattle area*
*(206) 728-0123*

## AUGUST

## SeaFair Celebration continued

*(206) 728-0123*
*Hydroplane Races*
*Torchlight Parade*
*U.S. Naval Fleet Arrives at Elliott Bay*
*SeaFair U.S. Navy Blue Angels Air Show*

## SEPTEMBER

## Bumbershoot

*Seattle Center/Seattle*
*(206) 684-7200*

## Western Washington Fair

*Puyallup*
*(253) 845-1771*

## OCTOBER

## Oktoberfest

*Poulsbo*
*(206) 682-8322*

## NOVEMBER

## Yulefest

*Nordic Heritage Museum/Ballard*
*(206) 789-5707*

## DECEMBER

## Christmas Celebration

*Seattle*
*(206) 623-0340*

## Christmas Display at Volunteer Park Conservatory

*Seattle*
*(206) 684-4075*

## KING 5 Winter Fest

*Seattle Center/Seattle*
*(206) 684-7200*

## Times Square of the West New Year's Eve Celebration

*Seattle*
*(206) 443-9700*

# Index

# Special thanks to:

Barbara Sullivan is the author of *Seattle Picnics: Favorite Sites, Seasonal Menus, and 100 Recipes* from Alaska Northwest Books. She lives in Seattle with her husband and four children, where she proved that in Seattle it is possible to meet, date, and marry that special someone.

Sullivan was born in Dubuque, Iowa and has worked as a nurse in Minnesota, Pennsylvania, and Missouri before moving to Washington. During her many moves and travels, she has collected food and family lore.

Currently she is Coordinator of Learning Resources at Seattle University's School of Nursing where she puts her love of computers to use.

Stephen R. Whitney is the author of *Nature Walks in and Around Seattle* and *A Field Guide to the Cascades and Olympics*. He currently works as a technical writer for the Microsoft Corporation.